The thrilling biography of one of the most famous Americans. Thomas Jefferson's boyhood in colonial Virginia, his education as a lawyer, his career as a member of the house of burgesses, governor of Virginia, minister to France, secretary of state, and president make an inspiring story.

"*We hold these truths to be self-evident: that all men are created equal; that they are endowed by their Creator with certain unalienable rights, that among these are life, liberty, and the pursuit of happiness; that to secure these rights, governments are instituted among men, deriving their just powers from the consent of the governed . . .*"

by *Clara Ingram Judson*

Illustrated by ROBERT FRANKENBERG

Thomas Jefferson

Champion of the People

Follett Publishing Company CHICAGO

89

LIBRARY OF CONGRESS CATALOG CARD NUMBER: 52-3101

Books by Clara Ingram Judson

Abraham Lincoln, Friend of the People

Andrew Carnegie

Andrew Jackson, Frontier Statesman

Benjamin Franklin

Bruce Carries the Flag

Christopher Columbus was a Sailor (1964)

George Washington, Leader of the People

The Lost Violin

Michael's Victory

The Mighty Soo

Mr. Justice Holmes

Petar's Treasure

Pierre's Lucky Pouch

Reaper Man, The Story of Cyrus Hall McCormick

St. Lawrence Seaway

Sod-House Winter

Theodore Roosevelt, Fighting Patriot

Thomas Jefferson, Champion of the People

For Younger Readers

Abraham Lincoln

Christopher Columbus

George Washington

Author's Foreword

A SCENE OF BEAUTY stretches around a small mountaintop near Charlottesville, Virginia. One looks west and north to the violet blue of the Blue Ridge Mountains; south and east is the deep green of forests. Crowded highways, honking motors, have vanished, hidden by enveloping green. The time might be now—or two centuries ago, when young Tom Jefferson and his friend Dabney Carr climbed to this place and Tom decided that here, someday, he would build his home.

That was an odd choice. People lived by rivers, then, for rivers were the highways of the eighteenth century. Standing in that place, one wonders whether some inner urge told Thomas Jefferson that he needed to be high to dream the dreams that would help his country to freedom.

Mountains have long been associated with man's spiritual progress. Moses brought a new code of law from a mountain. David sang his songs on the hills. The Beatitudes were spoken to people gathered on a mountain. And from this high place in Virginia a man went forth to bespeak life, liberty, and a chance for happiness for all people.

As one turns from the enchanting vistas, Thomas Jefferson seems to be at Monticello, a tall, rangy, friendly man, coming across the lawn to greet his visitors with a welcoming smile, his favorite gray coat, green waistcoat and stockings, blending with the woodland scene. The beauty he created in brick and stone, lawn and garden, is vivid and real. Every American, every lover of liberty can rejoice that now this place is open to all people.

There, at the corner, is honeymoon cottage, there the lawn where the children played. Here is the entrance where Patsy and her papa climbed into the phaeton and set off for Philadelphia, for Paris, for Washington City. Was that so long ago? Standing there, it seems but a yesterday.

The spell of Jefferson's presence is equally vivid as one reads his letters. And as I came to know him well, I learned the reason why.

Thomas Jefferson is a living, contemporary spirit, needed now perhaps even more than in the early days of our republic. For Jefferson, of all our great leaders, saw the ever-present challenge of freedom. He knew that it could be lost by selfishness and inertia; knew that each generation must earn its own freedom by dedicated vigilance. The urge to bring his philosophy of government, his ideal of freedom, his faith in man, to young Americans became a driving force that persisted until this book was written.

Many people and organizations have generously helped me in the research for this work. I feel especially indebted to The Public Library of Evanston, Illinois, and to Louise Borchelt and Florence Davison of the staff; to the University of Virginia and William H. Wranek, director of University News Service; to the Virginia Historical Society of Richmond, Virginia, and Clayton Torrence, director; to Colonial Williamsburg and Arthur Pierce Middleton, director of research; to Deering Library, Northwestern University, The Pennsylvania Historical Society of Philadelphia; and to my daughter Mary Jane (Mrs. Kingsley L. Rice), who was my companion on the journey to Monticello and the Jefferson country.

Evanston, Illinois
April 28, 1952   *C. I. J.*

Thomas Jefferson

Champion of the People

chapter one

The Little White Schoolhouse

AUTUMN SUNSHINE drifted through the pines and maples and made bright patches on the lawn. The pupils in the little white schoolhouse cast wistful glances through the window when the master was not watching. Tuckahoe plantation in this year 1750 had many choice places for play: the gardens, the stables, the riverbank. The children longed to be free.

The tall black-clad schoolmaster bent over the desk of the youngest child, inspecting his writing.

"I shall show you once more, Thomas," he said sternly; "so listen carefully." He set the quill pen in proper position between the boy's thumb and forefinger. "Raise your wrist. Rest your hand lightly—so. Move your arm from your shoulder. Now write your name."

Painstakingly the boy formed the letters

Thomas Jefferson

Writing was hard when the master loomed above him.

"U-um, you are doing better," the man conceded. "Penmanship is important. Write your name fifty times. Then study your reading lesson." Thomas sighed with relief when the teacher moved on.

Thomas Jefferson, Thomas Jefferson—he had written his name six times when a new sound made him pause to listen. Swift running footsteps were nearing the schoolhouse.

"Mary! Tom!" the excited voice of Jane Jefferson called. "You are to come to the house! Quickly!"

"You forget yourself, Jane!" The schoolmaster faced her angrily as she paused at the door. "And you are late. Surely you have not been practicing your spinet all this time?"

"I had just finished, sir, when Mother gave me the message," Jane said. "We are to come. Father is here."

"Father!" Thomas rose abruptly. "May I go, sir?"

The master frowned, and his fingers itched for the switch Mrs. Jefferson did not allow him to use.

"Well, go," he answered, grudgingly.

Thomas dashed from the schoolhouse, followed by his sisters and cousins. They ran across the lawn and around to the side of the great white house. There they saw a cheerful confusion of horsemen, stableboys, and house servants unloading saddlebags.

"Father!" Thomas cried and threw himself against tall, vigorous Peter Jefferson. "You're home!"

"So I am!" For an instant the man held his only son close. Then he drew back and looked at the lad. "Hair red as ever," he chuckled. "Freckles show you have been outdoors as you should. But you are taller—not yet eight, are you, Son? And how clean you are! Or perhaps I am so used to hunter's clothes and the dirt of camping that decent things look remarkable."

"Did you see bears and wolves this time, Father?" the boy asked, his eyes bright with anticipation.

"Don't delay your father with questions, Thomas," Mrs. Jefferson called from the doorstep. Then she turned to a servant. "Take the bags to the study and show the gentlemen to their rooms. Dinner will be served soon."

Thomas turned and saw that several men had come with his father. He followed them into the house and saw that it, too, was astir with excitement.

Maids were setting the table in the big dining room. Other maids ran to and fro from the outdoor kitchen, where the head cook was in a flutter of preparation. Visitors were an everyday matter in colonial Virginia. But when the master of the house returned from a long absence, bringing guests, the cook's best efforts were expected.

Soon the family and visitors were seated at the long table, with the children around one end and the grownups at the other.

"Five of these are mine." Peter Jefferson waved his hand toward the children as he spoke to Joseph Fry, seated at his right. "The others are William Randolph's—the orphans who were put under my care, as you may remember."

"I heard of William's dying request," Fry said. "Not every man would leave his own plantation to care for the heirs and farms of a friend and relative. I thought it good of you."

Peter turned the compliment aside with a remark about their journey, and the children settled to eating. The dinner was delicious, and Mrs. Jefferson was so intent upon her guests that she did not once say "Careful!" or "No more of that!"

The visitors stayed overnight, and it was not until the next afternoon that Thomas found his father alone. He was sorting letters and papers at his table in the study.

"Did you find the line, Father?" Thomas asked eagerly.

"The line?" Jefferson was puzzled.

"Yes. Mother said that you and Mr. Fry were finding a line."

"Oh!" The man's eyes twinkled, but he did not laugh. "Yes, Joseph Fry and I went to find the line, the boundary, between Virginia and North Carolina. It is not the kind of line one brings home. It goes on a map. Look, Tom."

The big man searched through his papers till he found a certain sheet. He held it up for his son to see as he pointed.

"No one knew where Virginia ended and North Carolina began; so, with our men, Fry and I made a survey. We climbed mountains and swam rivers to get information for a new map. Here is the line—see?" His finger moved across the sheet, which was covered with lines and notes.

"Our expedition turned out to be a big task, Son, though no harder than surveying the boundary of the Fairfax lands on the Northern Neck. We shall send our new map to London, and Thomas Jeffrys, geographer to the king, will publish it."

"Did you sleep in a hollow tree, Father?" Thomas asked. "The stableboys say you did once."

"Oh, we did worse than that this time." Jefferson laughed. "The wolves were so hungry that we dared not risk a hollow tree. We climbed high and tied ourselves to branches so we should not fall while we slept. We kept fires going around the tethered horses; but even so, on two nights the wolves surrounded us, and we had to fight it out." Thomas's eyes grew big.

"Surveying frontier land is exciting business, Tom, with wild beasts, snakes, and swamps for hazards," Jefferson went on. "Three times we floundered in swamp mire. I'll tell you more at supper. I must work now."

Before long, Peter Jefferson went away again. This time he inspected his own and the Randolph farms and planned work.

For several months life at Tuckahoe went on about as usual. Thomas's writing improved, and he learned to enjoy reading.

He studied arithmetic and soon caught up with his sisters and cousins, though all but Martha were older.

Then one day at dinner, the spring when Thomas was nine, Peter Jefferson pushed back his chair and remarked, "Well, I think we'll move home next week."

"Home?" Thomas was astonished. "Isn't this home?" He looked around the paneled room, into the handsome parlor, through wide windows onto beautiful grounds. "Isn't it, Father?"

"No," Jefferson answered. "I thought you knew that this is a Randolph plantation. Of course you were a baby, only two, when we came here. Our home is Shadwell on the Rivanna, sixty-five miles west of here. Now that the Randolph cousins are older, they do not need us."

"Sister and I are to stay at Aunt's, and Brother will go to Latin school," one of the cousins said, proud of knowing.

The children thought the move an adventure. The whole plantation was busy with preparations. House servants packed linen, silver, clothing, and books. The blacksmith put new shoes on the horses, and the coachmaker installed new leather strips for springs. The schoolmaster left, and relatives came for the Randolphs.

At last all was ready. Mrs. Jefferson and her four daughters climbed into the coach. The door was slammed, the driver cracked his whip, and off went the double teams, down the tree-lined drive to the Williamsburg highway.

Thomas on a small horse and his father on a big one rode close behind the coach, ready to help if it mired in a creek.

Behind them trailed a long cavalcade of wagons carrying house servants, field hands, and their children, along with the furniture and baggage.

Thomas liked Shadwell the first minute he saw it. The

grounds sloped down to the river, and the house, though not elegant like Tuckahoe, had a comfortable look. To the east, across the river, was a rolling plain, and beyond that a small rounded mountain, different from the higher peaks back of the house.

"Perhaps Father will let me climb that little mountain soon," he thought. "I shall ask him." He turned and looked westward where the sun was setting behind the Southwest Mountains and, between two peaks, got a glimpse of the distant Blue Ridge. He was entranced with the mountains and glad that school was not to begin for a while. He wanted to explore this new place with his father.

But Peter Jefferson had little time for mountain climbing that busy spring. Duties called him away often, even here. He was justice of the peace at Charlottesville, a nearby village. And he was colonel for the county and in charge of militia, volunteer troops who kept in practice in case there should be Indian raids.

The real frontier was a hundred miles west, and nearby Indians were quiet. But the county thought it wise to keep up some defense. Indians were friendly to Peter Jefferson. The chiefs of various tribes often stopped by on their way to do business with the colony at Williamsburg.

Between his many duties, Peter Jefferson taught his son to ride well and to swim his horse across a stream. The next summer he taught him to paddle a canoe and to portage. Then he gave him a canoe for his very own.

"You are not to daydream when you are canoeing, Tom," he cautioned the boy. "You must keep a sharp watch for logs and tree roots and rocks. You might ruin your canoe on such things."

"Suppose I hit something, Father, and you are away," Thomas asked anxiously. "Who shall I have fix it?"

"Tom Jefferson!" his father exclaimed, annoyed. "Do your own mending! That's the way a boy learns!"

Thomas flushed, and the freckles showed vividly across his nose. He never forgot his father's words.

One summer a visitor at Shadwell had a violin, and Thomas was fascinated with the tunes the man played after dinner. The next time Peter Jefferson went to Williamsburg, he brought back a violin and spare strings.

"Maybe you can teach yourself to play, Tom," he said as he unpacked the instrument. "Your sister Jane will help you. She knows scales and has an ear for tunes."

Jane Jefferson could read music, too; so the two studied together daily, Jane playing the harpsichord and Tom the violin. Often he took his violin with him when they went to the woods to hunt plants and flowers for Jane's botany collections. When they rested on a log, he played and she sang folk songs, hymns, and psalm tunes. They liked the psalm tunes best.

In the winter Thomas attended Latin school some twelve miles away from home. The roads were so bad that Thomas and several other boys boarded with the schoolmaster, Reverend William Douglass. Peter Jefferson paid sixteen pounds a year for the five seasons that Thomas attended there.

Douglass was a Scotsman with a modest education. He taught the boys Greek, Latin, and French, as well as reading, writing, and arithmetic. Thomas liked school well enough; but he liked being at Shadwell better.

One summer the Cherokee Indian chief, Ontasseté, a friend of Peter Jefferson, came by. With two companions he made an

overnight camp at Shadwell. When Jefferson and Ontasseté finished their business talk, the chief stalked to the river and inspected Thomas's canoe, tied up there.

"Bad!" he grunted as he balanced the paddle on his hand.

"Oh, it answers well enough," Jefferson said casually. "Show the chief how you can paddle, Tom."

The boy had been standing near, fascinated by the chief's beads and feathers. He ran to his canoe, jumped in, and pushed off. Ontasseté watched critically; then he turned and spoke to Jefferson. Though Thomas could not hear the words, he could tell that the chief was not pleased. He sat tall, held the paddle well, and did his best. When he came back to shore, the men had gone. He could not find out what was wrong.

Some days later the chief came by on his return journey. He presented Thomas with a beautifully balanced paddle.

"Yes, he means it for you," Peter Jefferson assured Tom when the boy hesitated. "He says you paddle well, but the paddle I gave you is no good." Jefferson grinned.

Thomas ran to the canoe to try out his gift. This time the chief was pleased.

"Bring boy next time," Tom heard Ontasseté say, and Jefferson promised. But the right time for that journey never came. Days were full of work and play, of study and music, of hunting and long tramps. Months passed swiftly.

The summer that Thomas was fourteen, disaster came to the happy family at Shadwell. Peter Jefferson, a strong, vigorous man of fifty, was taken sick, and died.

Thomas could not believe the words when he was told. He slipped away from the frightening confusion at the house and climbed high on Peter's Mountain, the peak behind Shadwell, where he had hunted with his father. When he could climb no more, he sat on a log and buried his face in his folded arms, weighed down by his first sorrow.

"I am all alone," he told himself, forgetting mother, sisters, little brother, relatives, and friends.

"What shall I *do?* I have no one!" He seemed to know that this day his happy boyhood world had ended.

chapter two

Young Thomas Jefferson

DAYS PASSED before Thomas began to take part in the life around him. Gradually he began to read his father's beloved books, ride a favorite trail, or tune his fiddle to accompany Jane at the harpsichord. The household, with his mother, six sisters, and baby brother, Randolph, was astir from morning until night; and the young master had duties.

Thomas was comforted when he found that his father had made careful plans for his future. At the age of twenty-one he was to have his choice of property.

"I shall choose Shadwell," he said quickly, when the lawyer read the will. "But what will Randolph have?"

"Better wait until the time for decision arrives," the lawyer advised. "Your father had large holdings in land and slaves. Randolph will have plenty, and your sisters will each have an inheritance, too. Likely your father thought you would choose this place; that is fitting for the older son."

"Your father also made plans for your education." the lawyer continued. "He had always regretted his own lack of schooling; he was determined that you should have the best that he could give you. He had planned to send you to the Reverend Maury's Latin school this fall. There you can learn Greek, Latin, French, and classical literature and be with boys of good families."

"Father had spoken of the Latin School," Thomas said. "I am glad to do what he had planned."

The Reverend James Maury was of French Huguenot descent. He had been in Virginia a long time and had studied at the College of William and Mary in Williamsburg. His school, located some fourteen miles from Shadwell, was thought to be the best in the Piedmont area.

Virginia at this time had two groups: Tidewater families whose plantations were along the great rivers, the Potomac, Rappahannock, York, and James; and the Piedmont folk who lived west, on the higher plateau near the mountains. The sons of Tidewater planters were usually sent to Europe for their education. Piedmont boys were more likely to be sent to Maury.

Each year some planters moved westward, leaving their worn-out farms for the virgin soil nearer the mountains. They carried with them traditions of culture and the custom of educating their sons. Thomas's Tuckahoe cousin boarded with Maury; and a new friend, Dabney Carr, was also a boarder.

Maury had the largest library Thomas Jefferson had ever seen: about four hundred books of history, literature, religion, and philosophy, a word that Thomas found included books on botany, zoology, and other sciences.

The boys who had been there earlier showed Thomas their collections of fossils and butterflies and flowers. Thomas was fascinated.

"I like this place," he told the boys. "My sister Jane and I have made collections, but these are better." He thought this school was going to be worth the twenty pounds it cost.

Dabney Carr became Thomas's best friend; he went with him to Shadwell for Christmas. The clatter of their horses on the driveway brought the whole family to greet them. Stableboys raced for the honor of taking the horses.

"La! You have grown!" Mrs. Jefferson exclaimed proudly. She caught at her son's coat and held him firmly while she looked him over. "Your hair needs cutting, though. Your freckles are pale—are you studying too hard, Son?"

"I ride every day, Mother; you should not worry. All the boys have horses. We follow mountain trails on horseback or afoot. Is dinner ready? We're hungry, Mother."

The house was full of sisters, relatives, and friends; and

days went by quickly. Mornings the boys usually rode. After-noons Thomas spent time with Jane. He showed her how to improve her collections, and they practiced their music.

"Tomorrow Dabney and I plan to ride up my mountain," he remarked one day as Jane put her botany collection away. "I'll bring you some new leaves—that's a promise."

The next morning was clear and fine when Dabney and Thomas turned their horses south, swam the river, and rode the three or more miles to "Tom's Mountain." The rounded crest was so wooded that one could hardly get a view.

"We have to climb a tree—that tall one is the best," Thomas said. He tied the bridle rein to a sapling and shinnied up a tall walnut, with Dabney close at his heels.

"Look now!" he ordered, when the two were astride a branch. He waved his hand at the distant scene as though it was his own special possession. South and east the vast forests of the Piedmont rolled like a sea of green. West the tiny village, Charlottesville, lay between mountains, its roofs whitened with a light snow. To the north was Peter's Mountain, higher than Tom's, and beyond it, the Southwest Range.

"This is the most beautiful place in the world," he said.

"You haven't seen much of the world yet," Dabney teased. "I'm getting down to eat." Dulcey had given them a snack, and it would taste fine after this climb.

After vacation, Thomas rode a young horse back to school, a horse he meant to train.

One bright day in February Dabney suggested that Thomas

should try out his mount in a race with several other horses.

"Tom will never race that horse," scoffed one lad.

"Not that slow animal he brought back," said another.

"I'll race any time Dabney chooses," Thomas said, annoyed.

"You'll lose, Tom," Dabney warned. "You'll hate that."

Thomas chuckled. The boys eyed him, frankly puzzled.

"You set the time, Dabney," he said, cheerfully.

"Set it yourself, Tom. Any time you want to get beaten!"

"You bring this on yourself," Thomas announced. "I'll race you the thirtieth of this month."

"Done!" the boys shouted. "You daren't back out now, Tom. You set the day yourself."

Several days went by, and each afternoon Tom went out on his horse. The boys were amused; no training would put speed into that creature, not in time for this race.

Then, one morning, the Reverend Maury turned the calendar, and a new month, March, headed the page.

"But sir," Dabney said, when his upraised hand got attention, "yesterday was only the twenty-eighth!"

"True enough," the master agreed. "And now it is March. You seem to have forgotten that February has twenty-eight days; this is not leap year."

Dismayed, Dabney sat down; the others tried to hide their chagrin. Thomas looked disgustingly smug, they thought; they would make him pay for this. But that race was never run. After spring vacation Thomas rode back on a spirited, well-trained horse.

Dabney often visited Shadwell. Mrs. Jefferson thought that a boy who had six sisters and a small brother needed a boy to play with, and the two were congenial. They fished and swam; they went canoeing and explored the forest. Neither cared much for actual hunting to kill, but they liked the adventure of tramping a forest trail.

At Mrs. Jefferson's request, Thomas's guardian sent a dancing master to Shadwell while Dabney was there in the summer. Mr. Inglis taught them fashionable steps used in Williamsburg. Mrs. Jefferson thought that social graces were a necessary part of an education.

That summer and the next, Thomas and Dabney often thrust favorite books into their pockets, took a snack from the kitchen, and spent the day on Tom's mountain. They had found a tiny clearing among the trees, and there they stretched out to read and talk.

"Someday I shall build a house here," Thomas remarked.

"Silly!" Dabney scoffed. "Build on a mountain? How would you get stuff up here?"

"Oh, I'd manage," Thomas said, dreamy-eyed with his idea.

"Manage," scoffed Dabney. "You'd have to build a road, you'd have to lug everything you used—and wouldn't that be a nice chore. Cost a lot, too."

"But worth it," Thomas said. "Look, Dabney!" He rolled over and sat up. "Think of being on a mountaintop every day. Of seeing this every morning—"

"This isn't such a wonderful mountain. Lots are higher!"

"Yes, that's why I like this one. It's a little mountain, but it has a big view. I shall live here when I'm grown."

"I declare maybe you will," Dabney said. Thomas's eyes were shining; his face seemed to glow. "You really mean it, don't you, Tom?"

"I do, indeed!" He flashed a smile at Dabney. Thomas was not considered handsome; but when he smiled like that, Dabney had a warm, happy feeling for his friend.

"But this summer the mountain is just for you and me," Dabney said. "Maybe, when we are old men and die, we shall both be buried under this very oak."

"That's a promise," Thomas said. "Now where's that Shakespeare? If we are to finish *Henry VIII* today we'd better get on with it."

Christmas vacation of 1759, the winter that Thomas Jefferson was sixteen, he went to a house party at the home of Colonel Dandridge, in Hanover County, the second county east of Albemarle, where Shadwell was located. This was quite an event, and a long ride, too. Dulcey had taken pains with his clothes; lace ruffles were well pressed, his best satin suit fitted well, and his saddlebags were tightly packed with changes.

Thomas was about to ride off when he remembered his violin.

"Fetch it quickly, Caesar," he ordered.

"Can't you ever leave that fiddle?" his mother asked. "You will be dancing with pretty girls, Thomas. You will have no time for fiddling."

But Caesar got the violin. Thomas hung the light case around his neck.

"You never can tell what I may do, Mother," he said, grinning at her cheerfully. And, with Caesar, he galloped away.

At first Thomas was shy in this large group of young people. They seemed to know each other, and he alone was a stranger. But he danced well, and the girls liked his manners.

The next morning another guest arrived, a stranger to Thomas. He was shabbily, indeed carelessly, dressed in coarse hunting clothes. Mrs. Jefferson had said that everyone at the party would be very elegant. The newcomer was older than most, too. Thomas guessed that he must surely be twenty-five. But he was certainly popular; he was greeted joyously.

"Tom, you know Patrick Henry, don't you?" Colonel Dandridge said.

"I believe I have not the pleasure." Thomas bowed formally.

"You will know each other soon," one of the guests said casually. "Patrick fiddles, too. With both of you here, we can dance all day and night!"

In the drawing room Patrick went straight to the spinet.

"You've a good fiddle," he said, inspecting Thomas's without ceremony. "Let's have a tune."

Thomas couldn't resist that. They played until they were dragged to dinner. Patrick did not know classical music, in which Jane had given her brother training. But he had a keen ear and could follow any tune Thomas played. In the evening Patrick was commandeered for charades, for he was the best mimic at the party. But otherwise the fiddles were going steadily.

An evening later a pretty girl came up to Thomas.

"You fiddle all the time, Tom," she pouted. "You should be dancing."

"You do not lack gallants to dance with you," Thomas replied, smiling, "while I have but one fiddle!" Amused, she accepted a partner and danced off.

After dinner the ladies left the table. Thomas heard talk about college—the College of William and Mary, at Williamsburg. He asked questions and got a good deal of information.

"I think I should like college," he remarked.

"Of course you'll like it," the young man next to him said. "Better make your application soon if you want to attend the spring term."

Thomas thought this good advice; so on the way home from Hanover he stopped at Colonel Peter Randolph's to discuss the matter, and when he got to Shadwell he wrote to his other guardian, John Harvie.

> Shadwell, January 14, 1760

Dear Sir,

I was at Col. Peter Randolph's about a fortnight ago, and my schooling falling into discourse, he said he thought it would be to my advantage to go to the College, and was desirous I should go, as indeed I am myself for several Reasons . . . I shall get a more universal Acquaintance which may hereafter be serviceable to me; and I suppose I can pursue my Studies in the Greek and Latin as well there as here, and likewise learn something of the Mathematics. I shall be glad of your opinion,

And remain, Sir,

Your most humble servant,

Thomas Jefferson, Jr.

The "Jr." was used to avoid confusion with an older cousin of the same name.

Thomas sent the letter off and waited impatiently for an answer. His thoughts were constantly on college and what he hoped to learn and do there.

chapter three

In the Class of 1762

A FAVORABLE DECISION about college came sooner than Thomas had dared expect, and in the late winter he left Shadwell for Williamsburg. His saddlebags were crammed with books, a portfolio of music, and his best clothing. Jupiter, his body servant, journeyed with him, as befitted a wealthy young gentleman of colonial Virginia.

Thomas had never seen a city; Charlottesville was a tiny village, only a few houses and a blacksmith shop. So he was excited when they arrived on the main street of Williamsburg.

"Maybe we better be findin' your kin," Jupiter suggested.

"Time enough for that," Thomas Jefferson said. "First I shall ride up and down this handsome street—it must be a hundred feet wide—and the mud not nearly as deep as on the highway!"

They turned their horses and rode the length of the mile-long Duke of Gloucester Street. They saw Raleigh Tavern, with its sign swinging in the breeze and many horses tied at the hitchrack. They passed shops: the printer, wigmaker, and metalworker—all enticing, Thomas thought. They came to the Green, a wide grassy strip on their right, leading to the red-brick palace beyond handsome iron gates. They saw Bruton Parish Church and more shops, and at last came to the college campus.

The city had a thriving look; the French and Indian War was at long last ended, and the colony prospered. Rich planters as well as burgesses brought their families to share gay social life at the capital. The rain of yesterday had stopped, and box-wood hedges were fragrant; white frame houses looked clean; already the lawns were bright green, and jonquils and pansies were blooming.

His first curiosity satisfied, Thomas found Peyton Randolph's house and paid his mother's respects to her relatives. After a big dinner there, talk turned to college.

"You'd better stay with us, Cousin," his host invited. "The college is in a quarrel with the president, and I hear the food is bad. Scraps for supper. Pudding only once a week, and meat when you get it! If the Virginians were allowed to run it, things would be different. But what does the Bishop of London care about us?"

"Thank you, sir," Thomas answered. "But I'll take my chances. How many pupils are there now?"

"Less than a hundred all told—there are four schools in those buildings, Tom. The divinity school for parsons; the school for Indians—only a few attend that now; the school of philosophy, for general education in the arts. You enter that. Then there is a school for younger boys. Mann Page sends his son there. You will meet John; he enters the older group with you."

The next morning Thomas enrolled, and arranged for entrance examinations. Then he walked along the colonnade on the garden side of the largest building. Posted on the wall were printed rules for each of the four schools. Thomas paused and read what would be expected of him.

> 1. ...no scholar...do keep any race horse at ye College or be concerned in making races...
> 2. ...no scholar...do presume to appear playing or betting at ye billiard or gaming tables...or keeping fighting cocks.
> 3. ...no scholar...do frequent or be seen in ye ordinaries in or about town except as they be by their relatives.

"You see, they aim to keep us straight," a voice at Thomas's shoulder said. "No need to read all that—it merely forbids lying, bad manners, and quarreling. We are told to report facts if we see students breaking rules."

"This place must be very strict," Thomas remarked. "But that will not bother me. I came here to study."

"And you a Randolph?" His companion chuckled.

"You know me?" Thomas asked, surprised. "I have not the honor of your acquaintance."

"Your pardon. I'm John Page, of Rosewell." He referred to the great Page plantation across the York River. "Your cousins told me you were coming. We are to be in the same class." The two young men strolled off, chatting.

Thanks to Maury's careful training, Thomas passed his examinations and entered with advanced standing. He got a room at the college and settled down to study advanced Greek and Latin, French, Italian, mathematics, history, and literature. Sundays he sat in the south gallery reserved for students at Bruton Parish Church.

But the attractions of a town enticed Thomas away from his studies. Liking horses as he did, it was natural to go to the races; the track was back of the college. He dined with relatives; danced at balls at Raleigh Tavern; and attended the plays at the theatre by the Palace Green. He joined a secret society called the Flat Hats. It had no purpose but amusement, though the six members went about with a superior air of mystery.

Even his clothes changed. Thomas took to brightly flowered satin waistcoats, long ruffles, and huge silver buckles. His sisters would have been astonished at his foppish ways.

This gay life lasted until he went home for a short vacation in the late summer. Dabney Carr welcomed Thomas, and the two friends went to the mountain to have a good talk.

"I am going back with you, Tom," Dabney said. "Tell me, what is it like, this college?"

Thomas leaned back against the oak, feasted his eyes on the distant view, and recounted tales of parties, races, pretty girls, and fine dinners enjoyed in Williamsburg.

"But your books, Tom," Dabney asked. "What did you learn?"

Thomas turned and looked at his friend long and steadily.

"I wonder what has possessed me?" he said, as though waking from a dream. "I have wasted time—and money, too. I have no right to take money from my father's estate for folly. I have wasted a rare opportunity to work with Dr. Small. You will like him, Dabney. He came over from Scotland two years ago. Over there, he knew the famous botanist, Erasmus Darwin, and the inventor, James Watt. He knows so much, and he is a very good teacher."

"What subjects do you have with him?" Dabney asked.

"Until this year, philosophy and Greek. But now that the president is ill, Dr. Small teaches all of my courses. I hope to start German, too, this fall. Oh, Dabney, I can hardly wait to go back. I am going to surprise him this winter."

At home that evening, Thomas wrote to his guardian about his expenses. "The cost so far should be taken from my inheritance," he wrote. "It is not fair that it come from the estate."

But his guardian thought otherwise. "If you have sowed your wild oats thus, the estate can well afford to pay the bill." Thomas understood the implied meaning—wild oats were ended.

One of the first men Thomas saw when he returned to Williamsburg was the fiddler he had met at Colonel Dandridge's. He paused and asked Patrick Henry how he happened to be in town.

"I'm on a case," Patrick said, grinning. "I'm a lawyer."

"A *lawyer!*" Thomas Jefferson was thinking about study-ing law—and here was Patrick, actually practicing.

"Yes, I did it in a hurry," Patrick admitted. He had a gift for knowing what the other person was thinking. "I failed at my store, and I have to make a living for my wife and children; so I thought of law. I like to talk—why not argue cases? I asked myself. I read some books for three months—that's too long for books. Then I came here and was admitted to the bar. George Wythe wouldn't vote for me; he's a stickler for study. But I got in anyway!"

"You were here and didn't come to see me?" Thomas cried.

"Oh, I asked about you," Patrick admitted cheerfully. "But you are such a gay blade now . . ."

"Not anymore. That was last term. Now I'm working hard with Dr. Small. But you are to come and see me. Got your fiddle with you?"

Patrick nodded.

"Then come tonight. We'll have supper."

Patrick came then, and often afterward, for an evening of talk and music. Jupiter noticed that the man looked thin and hungry. He thought Jefferson could do with more than dormi-tory food, too; so he usually contrived a snack of cold meat and cornbread. Patrick ate every crumb in sight. Sometimes other young men dropped in, and the talk turned to colony matters and law cases. Patrick was more interested in people than in books, and he had many tales which he told in his smooth deep voice. The students were entranced with the stories Henry told.

"I think I'll study law," Thomas said to John Page, the morning after one of these evenings. "But I'll not be satisfied with the smattering that Patrick has picked up. Dr. Small says that George Wythe is one of the ablest jurists in all the colonies. He promises to introduce me to him soon. What do you think, John?"

John and Dabney both thought well of the idea, and they were vastly impressed when Dr. Small invited Thomas to call with him at the Wythe home facing the Green, beyond the church. Wythe drew the young redhead into talk and liked him.

"Your young friend has a quiet way," Wythe said later to Dr. Small, "but his manners are good, as a Randolph's should be, and his intelligence is above average. You say he plays the fiddle?"

"Quite well, it seems to me," Small answered.

"Um-m. I wonder." Wythe pinched his lip thoughtfully. "Governor Fauquier is looking for a new bow for his chamber quartet. Could you bring your young man next Tuesday?"

Thomas Jefferson felt miserably shy as he entered the palace gates with two middle-aged men of such distinction. His fiddle was slung over his shoulder, and extra strings were in his coat pocket. Tunes were running through his head—he hoped he'd not forget all he knew at the last minute! Then he stiffened his courage. He could not disappoint Dr. Small. One didn't.

The evening turned out well. Governor Francis Fauquier, successor to Dinwiddie of war days, was gracious and took them

to the parlor—the room with the harpsichord. Two or three
other men were there, and before Thomas had time to feel
tongue-tied, music was spread on racks and the small orchestra
—German flute, viola, and violin—began playing. Thomas
played second violin; he could read well, and he kept up with
the others.

"Bravo!" exclaimed the governor. "Never heard that
Handel done better—the first time we've played together, too!"
He wiped his brow with a silk pocket handkerchief and selected
another sheet of music.

They played until ten o'clock, when supper in the dining
room was announced. Altogether, it was quite an evening for
a seventeen-year-old. Thomas was thrilled and excited over his
good fortune.

As it turned out, that was only the first of many evenings
at the palace. The governor took a fancy to Dr. Small's student
and invited him often for playing and later to fashionable
concerts given at the palace.

In between, Thomas Jefferson studied faithfully. Dr. Small
had new ideas about teaching. Other professors expected students to memorize long sections, pages and pages, which they
were to recite. Dr. Small initiated what he called a "lecture
system." He talked to a group of students; and then, in their
rooms, the students wrote out what they remembered and understood of the lecture. Some days, Thomas wrote for hours.

"After I recall it and write it down, I remember better,"
he said to Dabney. "I think Dr. Small has a good way."

"Many don't agree," Dabney said. "They say it's too easy —this not memorizing each word."

Thomas grunted. "Dr. Small cares more about understanding than mere committing to memory. But there is no law against memorizing if we like. I think his method is good." He pulled his notebook toward him and went on writing.

During his college years Thomas was at home very little. The summer vacation was one month; he went home then and refreshed himself with hours on his mountain.

But the two other vacations were only a fortnight each— a short time for a trip of one hundred miles and return over bad roads. He contented himself with staying in Williamsburg or visiting John at Rosewell.

The end of college loomed only a month away when Dabney rushed into Thomas's room after dinner.

"A big delegation of Cherokees is camped outside of town," Dabney said. "They've come to bid their chief good-by. He is sailing for England to see the king about Indian business."

"Cherokees!" Thomas exclaimed. "My father knew a Cherokee chief—Ontasseté was his name. Father always meant to take me to see his camp, but we never got around to it."

"That's the man. A lot of us are going over this evening; better come along. It's said the old fellow is a real orator. He may put on a good act tonight; the moon is full."

"I believe I'll go," Thomas decided. He dipped his quill in the inkpot and wrote rapidly, finishing his notes.

Campfires glowed on solemn, copper-colored faces when

townspeople arrived at the temporary camp. Youths who had come to be amused stood silent and respectful in spite of themselves.

Presently an Indian rose and gathered his blanket around him, tall against the great moon rising above the forest. At his first word, Thomas whispered to Dabney.

"That's Ontasseté! I'd know his voice anywhere. My father called it smooth as honey."

The deep musical voice rolled out eloquently. Ontasseté's gestures and tones made his meaning plain even to those who understood no word of his language. He loved his people; he was journeying across the vast sea for them; he would tell the king their needs and wishes. The moon rose higher and spread a bright magic that held all in a spell.

When the voice stopped, Williamsburg folk slipped away, awed with what they had seen and heard.

"I'm glad we went, Dabney," Thomas said, as they walked back to the college. "I feel as though I had been with my father."

Months passed, and in April of 1762, shortly after his nineteenth birthday, Thomas Jefferson graduated from the College of William and Mary. The four-year course had taken him two years and one month. Now he looked toward a well-planned and very agreeable future.

chapter four

The Student at Law

ONE EVENING IN SPRING, Dr. Small, George Wythe, and young Jefferson strolled home after a concert at the palace. The wide Green seemed dark after the glow of many candles; the soft breeze was refreshing, for the rooms had been crowded with guests.

"The lilacs are fine this year," Dr. Small remarked. "To my notion the town is at its best in spring. Is it too late to come in for a talk, George?"

"It is never too late for that; come in, both of you," Wythe invited. "There is a bit of fire in the study."

They sat in comfortable silence for a few minutes before Wythe asked, "Something on your mind, William?"

"Yes," Dr. Small admitted. "Tom gets his degree Tuesday. I have been asking him, 'What next?'"

"And has he answered?" Wythe glanced at Thomas, smiling.

To the lawyer's surprise Small spoke for his friend.

"Tom says he plans to study law—with you, he hopes."

"With me?" Wythe had not expected that.

"Yes, sir, if you will have me," Thomas answered eagerly.

"I approve your decision to study law," Wythe said. "I hoped you would come to it soon. But I supposed you would study with Peyton Randolph. He is Attorney to the King and your mother's cousin. Edmund Pendleton is a fine lawyer, too, and your good friend."

There was no law school in Virginia. Young men "read law" under the direction of an established attorney. Thomas was pleased to know that Mr. Wythe had thought of his future.

"Thank you, sir," he said. "I appreciate my good fortune. But my first choice is to study with you."

"What would be your plan after graduation?" Wythe asked.

"When I leave college next week," Thomas began, "I could take lodgings in town; Jupiter can do for me nicely. I have some duties at home this summer. Perhaps after my studies are begun I could work at Shadwell instead of here."

"When you are settled in your lodgings," Wythe told him, "come and see me at my office. I am an exacting taskmaster, but you want to learn."

In a few days Jefferson called on Wythe. Most Williamsburg lawyers had a small office near the house; Wythe's was by the garden. After a brief greeting, the lawyer picked up a list of books that he had written out.

"Your first book must be Littleton's English Law with Coke's Commentaries." His manner was formal and businesslike; Thomas expected that, for they were now master and apprentice. "This is a basic work. Study it line by line until you understand it. I call it the lawyer's primer.

"Probably you have some of these books," he went on as he handed Thomas a list. "You can order the others at the *Gazette* office. I want you to continue your study of classics and philosophy. A lawyer needs general knowledge."

A glance at the list showed Jefferson that he knew several— Plato, Milton, Cicero, the Bible. Others were new to him. He resolved to look them up at once.

"You should attend the general court when it is in session," Wythe went on, "and the house of burgesses. Write down in a commonplace book your impressions of all you read and hear. This habit will force you to think about what you learn and will also give you a record."

"I like keeping a notebook," Jefferson said. "I did all through college."

"Now in a few days," Wythe added, "bring me a plan for

daily study. If you follow a well-planned day, you may study any place that is convenient."

As he bowed out and went to the *Gazette* to order his books, Jefferson felt assured and happy. He had begun his life career.

Jefferson brought in his program of study a few days later, and Wythe read it thoughtfully. Rise at five, earlier in summer. From then till eight read books on agriculture, botany, zoology,

chemistry, anatomy, and religion. Eight to twelve study Coke and Littleton. Twelve to one, politics; and in the afternoon, history. For lighter work, evenings, he listed rhetoric, oratory, literature, and languages. The whole was surely ambitious.

Wythe approved the program. He did not point out the omission of hours for eating and exercise, but that idea suddenly occurred to Jefferson.

"I shall run a mile into the country and back each afternoon," he said. "My father believed that running keeps a man fit. Soon I should take up Anglo-Saxon, I think, sir. English law comes from the Saxons, I have learned."

With this ambitious beginning, Jefferson settled down and worked hard. Jupiter put meals before him and fussed until he ate them. Invitations were refused. Some weeks later, books and papers were packed in saddlebags, and the two went home.

Dabney Carr was at Shadwell; the young men were nineteen now, and both studying law. When Thomas finished daily duties on the plantation, they took books and food to the little mountain and studied until dark. Thomas missed his friend when, after a time, Dabney had to leave to take a job.

Jefferson missed Williamsburg, too. He wrote to John Page:

"We rise in the morning that we may eat breakfast, dinner and supper, and go to bed again that we may get up in the morning and do the same. You never saw two peas more alike than our yesterday and today."

Back in Williamsburg in the autumn, Thomas alternated between a few days of gaiety and weeks of grinding study.

Wythe was pleased, but Williamsburg belles thought Thomas needlessly cruel. A tall, graceful dancer wasted on law books! He certainly did not need to work—he, the heir of a rich man.

When Thomas was twenty, he fancied himself madly in love with a pretty girl named Rebecca Burwell. He called her his "Belinda" and danced with her devotedly at the balls. Rebecca was a popular miss of sixteen—just the age when a girl in colonial Virginia expected to marry. Thomas Jefferson interested her; he was tall and nice-looking, even though a redhead and freckled. He stammered entrancingly when she dropped her long lashes; she loved the feeling of power he gave her.

As for Thomas, he was utterly and blissfully miserable. Should he propose to her? Or wait? He argued the question with John Page; they were talking of a trip to Europe and could hardly take a bride along.

As Thomas dressed for a fashionable ball at Raleigh Tavern one evening, he planned and rehearsed an elegant speech. Between dances he maneuvered Rebecca behind rose window-draperies in the Apollo Room. Then, suddenly, he forgot that beautiful speech!

"Belinda . . . I . . . er . . . " he improvised, "if I should sometime tell you . . . er . . . would you wait for me?"

"Wait!" Nothing was further from Belinda's practical intentions. She flounced from the curtained recess and gaily danced off with another man. Soon after, she married. Jefferson earnestly told himself that he was well out of it. He went at his law books with renewed vigor.

Jefferson was enjoying his hard work with Wythe. He studied each law, English or colonial, to get the heart of its meaning; this he wrote in his notebook. Often he paused, pen in hand, and wondered—was this a good or necessary law? Was it wise for the people? Then he would remind himself that his work now was to study, not to criticize laws on the books.

Two years after Thomas Jefferson began studying law, he celebrated his twenty-first birthday, April 13, 1764, at Shadwell. His mother had invited relatives and friends; the house was filled with visitors. To mark the day, he planted a double row of locust trees along the drive to the house. His family and the guests watched the setting of those saplings and wished him well. Then they went in to a great dinner.

The tall, quiet young man at the head of that birthday feast was being developed by various influences. Hardy frontiersmen brought out a sturdy boldness; from gentlemen in the palace drawing rooms he had learned social graces and the art of conversation. A deep love of nature gave him an eagerness to know sciences; and a joy in reading, fostered by his father, made long hours of study a satisfaction. Thomas Jefferson at twenty-one was a versatile, thoughtful, well-informed man of high character.

On this day Thomas Jefferson formally made his choice of land in his father's estate—the 2560 acres along the Rivanna which included Shadwell and his little mountain. He also inherited some 2500 acres in other locations, and many slaves. His mother had a life interest in the home; his sisters would have a cash inheritance on their marriage, and there was land for young Randolph. Peter Jefferson had provided for all his family, not merely for the eldest son.

Much of the Jefferson land was still wilderness, but Thomas at once took over the farming of cleared fields and, from that time on, had an income of his own. Shortly afterward, he was elected justice of the peace for Albemarle County and vestryman for his parish.

A few days after his birthday, Thomas asked Jane, Martha, and Dabney to climb his mountain. "I want to tell you something," he said.

"It's a nice little mountain, Tom," Martha, the practical one, said when they reached the crest.

"Not 'Little Mountain,'" her brother corrected her. "From this day its name is Monticello. I wanted you to know."

"You are just showing off your Italian," Dabney teased.

"Indeed, no!" Thomas flushed hotly. "I like the sound of the word—Monticello." He spoke it with the *ch* sound. "Some day I shall build a home of classical design on this very spot. I have seen drawings I like in the governor's library."

Martha and Dabney smiled. But Jane looked at him soberly. "I believe you will, Tom. And you will make it beautiful."

While he was making plans for planting and other spring work, Jefferson happened to think about harvest and the marketing that now would be his responsibility. Everything grown at Shadwell had to be hauled to Richmond—tedious and expensive business. But since the Rivanna was cluttered with rocks, Albemarle farmers had no choice but to go by road.

Jefferson resolved to explore. He took one of the hands with him in a canoe and paddled as far as possible. When rocks stopped him, he tied the canoe at the bank and waded in.

"I think these could be dislodged," he said. "Here! Give me a hand." Together they pulled, and the rock came loose. He tried several; none were too tightly embedded.

The next day he called on some of his neighbors and raised

a small fund for moving those rocks. By summer a channel in the river was open, and harvests were floated to market on rafts—a very practical improvement.

As soon as the actual work on the Rivanna was under way, Jefferson rode back to Williamsburg and continued his studies. Gradually he was taking his place among men. People called him "Mr. Jefferson" when they met him in the courts, the taverns, or the capitol.

Almost at once, Jefferson realized that the feeling toward England had changed during his weeks at home. Talk was no longer about the year-old Treaty of Paris but of the recent news. Prime Minister Grenville planned to raise money in the colonies to pay British debts. An act declaring his right to tax Americans had passed in Parliament. Grenville proposed to get the money by stricter customs duties and a Stamp Act taxing legal papers and newspapers.

Even loyal Tidewater Virginians felt they must protest. But the letter they wrote was mild, almost begging, in tone. Before any answer arrived, news came that the Stamp Act, too, had passed. It would take effect in November of 1765.

"This puts a different light on the matter," Wythe said. "The Act is now a law, and a law must be obeyed."

Many agreed with Wythe; others differed. The question was argued on street corners and by firesides in Williamsburg, Philadelphia, Boston, and at crossroads between.

Jefferson was reading his *Gazette* one morning when talk at the tavern began to swirl around him.

"I'm not interested in legal theories," he heard a man say. "I want to know what we can *do!*"

"Nothing!" someone answered. "The law is passed."

"But Parliament had no right to pass it!"

"The house of burgesses should take action!"

"How? They're helpless!" Angry words flew fast.

"Helpless?" Jefferson turned in surprise, for the last speaker had chuckled. He recognized a neighbor from Louisa County, not far from Shadwell.

"Hadn't you heard?" the Louisa man went on, relishing his news. "One of our burgesses resigned, and we're electing Patrick Henry to take his place. Pat's not helpless. Better watch him if you want to see fur fly!"

"Patrick Henry will not take a slap lying down!" someone said. A look of relief was seen on many faces.

When Henry arrived in Williamsburg, people watched him, sensing drama.

Henry promptly presented to the house of burgesses resolutions declaring that British Americans had equal rights with other British subjects; and that the people who paid taxes were the only ones who had a right to assess taxes. This principle, he asserted, was the very basis of political freedom. The resolutions were seconded, and Henry got up to speak for them.

Meanwhile, word that Patrick Henry was in action spread through the building, and a crowd gathered in the hall. Jefferson luckily got a place by the open door into the burgess room where he could see and hear everything.

The scene was like a play, Jefferson thought. Elegant Tidewater burgesses stared at the member from Louisa. Henry wore his usual shabby hunting clothes. His shoulders sagged, as always. His voice was low; men bent forward to hear.

But as Patrick Henry warmed to his subject, he seemed to grow tall. His eyes lighted with an inner fire; his voice deepened and was assured. Every word could easily be heard out in the hall. He seemed to weave a magic spell as his eloquence moved to its climax.

"Caesar had his Brutus; Charles the First his Cromwell; George the Third . . . " he was saying when shouts chilled the listeners.

"Treason! Treason!"

Henry hardly paused. " . . . may profit by their example!" Undaunted, he moved the adoption of his resolutions.

The room was silent; hearers dumb as though under a spell.

"Homer must have spoken like that," Jefferson whispered.

The resolutions passed by one vote. A frontiersman's eloquence had broken with tradition.

The next morning burgesses tried to change the vote. They were not successful.

Jefferson was thrilled, shocked, fascinated—and a little amused—at this dramatic lesson in politics. Then he settled down to his legal studies. For months, nothing happened about that Stamp Act. Affairs between nations moved slowly in the days of sailing ships.

In the summer of 1765, Jefferson went to Shadwell for the marriage of his sister Martha and Dabney Carr. This event pleased him; he often visited their modest home in Charlottesville, where Dabney had opened a law office.

Jefferson was still at home, attending to farm business and studying, when his beloved sister Jane became ill. She lived only a few days; her death was a bitter blow. He gathered up their music books and locked them in a cupboard; he shut the harpsichord and put away his violin.

"I cannot play without Jane," he said to his mother.

Shadwell seemed strange. Mary had been married for five years. Martha was in her own home—and now Jane, his loved companion, was gone. Elizabeth, the sister next to him, was simple-minded and cared only to roam alone. Lucy was entering her teens; and the twins, Ann and Randolph, were ten, not yet companions for a studious man of twenty-two.

As soon as Jefferson could rouse himself to travel, he and Jupiter went to Williamsburg. Work and the excitement of politics might help him to forget.

chapter five

The Young Attorney

JOHN PAGE and Thomas Jefferson did not take the grand tour of Europe as they had planned. As a consolation to himself, Jefferson went on a three-month journey to northeastern cities.

Spring planting was done when, on a sunny day in May, the family gathered to see him off. Jefferson was twenty-three when he took this first journey outside of Virginia.

"Are you sure Jupiter has packed all you need?" his mother called from the doorstep.

"I can buy in Philadelphia if I need anything, Mother."

"Oh, Tom, will you bring me something?" Lucy begged. "I should love to have a scarf from the city."

"I promise you!" he grinned at her. "And you shall have a present, too!" he promised the twins. "Good-by, now!"

Jefferson climbed into the chaise. The stableboy handed over the reins, Jupiter leaped onto his seat behind, and away they went—the horse tossing his handsome head and stepping high.

Driving in a chaise was more troublesome than Jefferson expected; he half wished he had planned to ride. But he was a skillful driver and he had a good horse. Somehow they managed the rutted trails, the swollen rivers and rocky fords, the pouring rains and many discomforts. Evenings at a farmer's home or small inn, Jefferson wrote long letters to John Page telling of his adventures.

Townsfolk were celebrating the repeal of the Stamp Act when they drove into Annapolis.

"They act like a wild mob!" Jefferson exclaimed to Jupiter. "Virginians will be glad to hear of the repeal. But they will not show it this way!" He paused on a side street until the shouting crowd had passed. Then he found lodgings and walked around the town.

Its fine location by the sparkling Chesapeake Bay seemed excellent; the capitol was handsome. But when he visited the assembly, he thought they were too informal. The contrast with Virginia's dignified house of burgesses made him eager to visit other cities and see people who had other ways and manners.

While driving through Maryland, Delaware, and Pennsylvania, Jefferson observed many new sights. Instead of Virginia forests, he saw open fields planted in clover, flax, and grains. He often stopped to talk with farmers about these crops.

"You Virginians will come to using crop rotation," one prosperous farmer told him. "Tobacco wears out the soil."

"We move on to other fields," Jefferson remarked.

"That does for a time, yes," the man agreed. "But you are getting more settlers. I hear of Germans and Scotch-Irish moving into the Shenandoah Valley. The time will come when you'll have to replant on your same fields."

"Mind telling me your plan of rotation?" Jefferson opened his notebook and wrote down the farmer's suggestions. "I shall try some of this next spring," he said gratefully.

Philadelphia enchanted Jefferson. Its nearly twenty-thousand people, its many homes and businesses, spread two miles along the river. Its well-stocked shops made it seem a different world from Williamsburg, which he had thought so important. He strolled about, admiring the capitol, observing the ways of Pennsylvanians, and shopping for gifts.

An Albemarle neighbor had given Jefferson a letter of introduction to the famous Dr. John Morgan. When he presented it Jefferson asked that the doctor inoculate him for smallpox.

"Sometimes inoculation proves dangerous," Dr. Morgan warned. "You have very little smallpox in Virginia—big cities are the danger points. Are you sure you want to take the risk?"

"Quite sure," Jefferson replied. "This is one of the reasons for my journey. I believe in prevention of illness."

"I shall ask my friend Dr. William Shippen, Jr., to attend you," Dr. Morgan decided. "He is a specialist in this new form of medicine." The inoculation was successful, and soon Jefferson went on to see New York.

After a stay in this smaller city, he sailed for home. This, he had decided, was wiser than the hard drive. He took Jupiter and his horse and chaise with him; they would drive home from Norfolk.

In a few weeks Jefferson was back in Williamsburg, studying law with fresh zest. Wythe and other friends were interested in his travels and in reports of his talks with men in other places.

The men who gathered around Wythe's fireside called themselves "Whigs." That century-old word stood for citizens who were for the rights of men and against the tyranny of kings. They still thought of themselves as British subjects, but they were concerned about the demands for taxes, and about other recent acts of Parliament.

Since the day when Patrick Henry's oratory had won votes for his bold resolutions, Virginia leaders had been worried. Men like Wythe and Randolph agreed that in theory British Americans had equal rights with the British who lived in England, but doubted whether it was wise to pass resolutions about it. The cautious men called themselves "conservatives" because they wanted to save all the good that was in the old ways.

"Liberal" followers of Patrick Henry challenged caution. They thought of themselves as broadminded and independent, not bound by the past. At this time, Jefferson listened to both points of view; he was both frontier planter and townsman.

Early in 1767, he passed the bar examinations entitling him to practice law in the county courts of Virginia and in the general court. This court met in Williamsburg each April and October; trials were held before the governor and the council.

Almost at once, Jefferson had a number of cases. His long study with Wythe was well known; probably no lawyer in the colony had had better preparation for legal work.

But Jefferson himself soon realized that in spite of fine training, he had certain handicaps. He did not really enjoy court work. He liked to dig into a hard case, discover evidence, and plan action in the quiet of his office. His voice, pleasant in conversation, soon wearied in court. He had neither liking nor talent for oratory, in which Dabney Carr and Patrick Henry excelled.

In his first year Jefferson had sixty-eight cases in the general court and many in county courts. In his years at law he worked in fifty-three of Virginia's fifty-seven counties. His cases had to do with debts, land grants, mortgages, trespass, and contested elections. Men liked and trusted him.

"Get Tom Jefferson to take your case if you can," word went around. "He's a good office lawyer; gets everything in order. If you need court work, Tom can get Henry or Carr to work with him."

"Jefferson won my fence fight for me," a planter said. "He got at the heart of the matter at once—won hands down!"

After the court closed in the spring of that year, 1767, Jefferson went to Shadwell and soon began planting on his mountain. He set out raspberries, currants, gooseberries, and other small fruits on the south slope. As he planned that work, he studied his mountaintop and the views, and a definite design for his home grew clear in his mind.

At this time most Virginia houses were quite simple in design and showed no special striving for architectural beauty. Thomas Jefferson admired classical buildings, and he had a deep admiration for the work of Palladio, the sixteenth-century Italian architect.

When he was at Shadwell that summer, Jefferson drew a plan for a house, inspired by Palladio's ideas. But it was original, too, for Jefferson adapted it to Virginia. When maples and dogwood turned red, he reluctantly put his drawings away and went to Williamsburg. His calendar was full of cases for the general court.

By the next spring, he had made working drawings for a handsome mansion and had figured the number of bricks needed for the main section and two wings. Details always gave Jefferson pleasure. His mind could hold great thoughts and everyday business, too.

On a day in May, 1768, Jefferson and a contractor went to the mountain to plan a start of the work.

"I want the whole top of the mountain cleared and leveled, Mr. Moore," Jefferson said. "I need a rectangle 250 by 500 feet."

"That's a big plot, Mr. Jefferson. The cost will be heavy."

"You will be properly paid in corn and wheat of this year's harvest," Jefferson promised. "I shall want the work finished by Christmas. I shall make my survey for the house then."

Moore strolled ahead and studied the lay of the land. "You'll have a fine view from here—but materials will have to be hauled quite a piece."

"I shall make the brick up here." Jefferson smiled at Moore's surprise. "We'll make our own nails and woodwork. Of course windows must be hauled. I have ordered those from

England. But, in the main, my people will do the work. I think it a good idea for men and women to know a trade. My people are learning, now."

"You'll face the house south?" Moore asked.

"No," Jefferson said. "Most houses are set with the compass, but mine is to look southwest and catch the best view of the mountains. I shall take advantage of my mountain slope and build terraces eighteen feet wide, running the short sides of this rectangle I speak of. These will be walks—but also the roofs of work buildings—the stables, carriage room, weaving rooms, smokehouse, and such. Nothing is to mar my view."

He took a bit of paper from his pocket and sketched a rectangle, open on one side, showing house and terraces.

"Never saw anything like that, Mr. Jefferson," Moore said. "It ought to be beautiful."

"Get your work done by Christmas, and I shall start building early next spring," Jefferson said as they left. "Already we are digging the cellar."

While this dream house was beginning upon the mountain, Lawyer Jefferson lived in comfortable lodgings in Williamsburg. Most of his friends were married, and he was a welcome guest in town and in many a plantation home. He worked hard; but he found time for pleasure, too. Young men were expert at chess, backgammon, and cards; young people danced and rode and went to plays, amateur and professional.

The palace was dark this fall of 1768, for the popular Governor Fauquier had died suddenly. Jefferson missed him and the happy evenings of music. Another governor would be sent over, but it was not likely that he would be the helpful friend Fauquier had been.

In place of chamber music, singing was the fashion at the moment. Young ladies played the harpsichord in turn, and the young men sang. Time had softened the sorrow of Jane's death enough so that Jefferson could again enjoy music. He bought a new violin, and he must have played many hours; his account books had frequent items for new strings.

But neither work nor play prevented Jefferson from keeping up with news from England.

"That Townsend Act will make trouble yet," a client remarked at the end of a conference, one day. "We'll not like a tax on glass, lead, and molasses any better than a Stamp Tax. Will England never learn?"

"I suppose you are reading John Dickinson's letters in the *Gazette?*" Jefferson asked, referring to a well known Pennsylvanian. "He wants us to behave like dutiful children who have received undeserved blows from a loved parent. Can you accept that?" The client chuckled.

"Sam Adams, in Boston, does not," he said. "But we Virginians ship only tobacco. We are not hit by all the taxes."

"We feel injustice just as keenly," Jefferson said quickly. "But you are right—New Englanders are more troubled by all this in their daily living." Graciously, he bowed his client out. Jefferson regarded disputes with England in a rather impersonal way. His own affairs were prospering.

chapter six

Burgess From the Uplands

IN THE SPRING OF 1769, when Thomas Jefferson was twenty-six years old, he went home to Shadwell to vote in a general election in Albemarle County. There was another reason for his going home: his friends had put him up as a candidate for burgess, and the custom of the time required a candidate to entertain the voters on the day of the election.

The Jefferson place looked beautiful that morning when he rode off to Charlottesville to vote. His five-year-old locust trees were heavy with bloom, and fragrant petals from the orchard drifted on the breeze like snow. The family and all hands were bustling about, and luscious odors from the barbecue were already making many a mouth water.

Early in the day it was seen that Jefferson had won the election. The voters cheered, much pleased, though the result was hardly a surprise. Peter Jefferson had been a burgess, and his son was now known to be an educated gentleman and a successful lawyer with many friends at the capital. Gaily they mounted and followed the new official to Shadwell to celebrate.

Talk flowed as visitors were made welcome.

"Albemarle has done well by itself today," a stout German from the Valley said. "We're lucky. Tom's the best lawyer in the colony; he owns five thousand acres and knows what a farmer needs, too."

"That's so," a neighbor answered. "Many a rich man would stay in Williamsburg and leave his farms to an overseer. Not our man! He's building a house in the county. I like that."

"He's kin to the Randolphs, but he puts on no airs," a cheerful Irish farmer remarked. "Me own father couldn't'a been kinder about that fence trouble I had."

"I hear even the new governor has noticed Tom," another said. "He has given him command of his majesty's horse and foot in Albemarle."

The new burgess went about among the men thanking them, making them at home. The great roasts were done to a turn. Children, black and white, ran errands and snatched delicious bits while Mrs. Jefferson, like a general, managed the feast from her chair by the front door. Young and old enjoyed that election celebration.

Soon after, Jefferson went to Williamsburg to begin his duties.

The new governor, Botetourt, had been in Virginia for some time before he called an assembly. He had made friends and was quite well liked, though some thought him too extravagant, since Britain was having trouble with debts.

For the opening of the assembly on May ninth, 1769, the governor drove to the capitol in an elegant coach drawn by six white horses. Crowds cheered; this was like the king, going to Parliament! But when the coach had passed, there were mutterings about royal airs. The governor went to the house of burgesses, where, shortly before, the new burgesses had taken the oath of office.

Botetourt was handsomely dressed in satin and laces. He mounted the rostrum and spoke gracious words of welcome to burgesses and council members in this, their first meeting. Then he retired, and the house elected Peyton Randolph as speaker and began regular business.

The first duty was to reply formally to the governor's greeting. Six burgesses, Jefferson among them, were appointed as a committee to write the letter; and they went into another room for this work.

"I suggest that Mr. Jefferson write the paper," Mr. Pendleton said, with a bow to the new member. "We all know the quality of his pen in legal writing." Others murmured approval. Jefferson took out paper and pen and began to write.

But when the result was read, Mr. Nicholas objected.

"That will hardly answer," Nicholas complained. "The work needs an experienced hand."

"Then write it yourself!" Pendleton exclaimed, annoyed. Jefferson was silent and miserable. His face flushed, and each freckle stood out boldly across his nose.

Nicholas's paper was accepted, and the committee returned. But Jefferson's misery was not so quickly ended. He felt he had failed—and at the very beginning of his political career. It was many hours before he could even think of the work at hand.

After a few days of routine business, the matter of taxes came up. Immediately the house was tense; a long-awaited crisis had come. But the debate was calm enough, and then the resolutions were passed. These declared that only they who paid the tax had the right to levy it; that colonists must be allowed to petition for correcting an injustice; and that a person should be tried in his own colony where he could get witnesses. The words were not exactly the same, but the principles were those Patrick Henry had spoken for, years earlier.

The governor prided himself on being a tolerant man, but the burgesses were too bold for him. He "dissolved" the assembly. This legal term meant more than merely ending a meeting. New elections must be held before burgesses could convene again. It was a drastic move for a new governor to make.

Nothing daunted, the burgesses marched to Raleigh Tavern, elected Randolph chairman of their meeting, and passed a new and even bolder motion. They pledged that after September first they would buy nothing from England! This, by men who bought all their luxuries and many of their comforts oversea! Washington, Henry, and Jefferson were among the signers; and every man who signed that pledge was re-elected.

Before the meetings ended Jefferson had come to feel acquainted with Colonel Washington, and he liked him. He also worked with Richard Henry Lee, who had been in the assembly for several years. Lee was not a lawyer but was well educated and open-minded. Jefferson had a gift for noticing men's abilities and character; such information was stored in his mind.

When summer came it was pleasant to go to the country and work with the men on the new house. That season they built a small brick house—one room about twenty feet square at the southeast end of the terrace. Some service buildings were finished, too; and the roof-terrace was a pleasant, dry place from which to watch the sunset.

It was well that the work went ahead so fast that summer, for during the following winter Shadwell took fire and burned to the ground. Jefferson was at Monticello at the time, and a slave ran all the way to bring the bad news.

"The house is all gone, Marster!" the man shouted, gasping. "Everything's gone!" Then the dark face lighted. "No, not everythin'—we saved your fiddle! We saved it!"

"But my books! My papers!" Jefferson was pale with shock. "My music!"

"They's all gone—jus' ashes, that's all!"

That library had cost Jefferson and his father more than two hundred pounds—a large sum in those days. Thomas himself had collected a good musical library.

"But I would rather have burned up twice the money and kept those books," he remarked to the slave, as they hurried back to Shadwell. "And my notes for law cases in the spring court! My garden books and accounts! It is a loss indeed!"

Jefferson had kept records of every penny, every case, every planting; he liked to set down facts. He kept an index so he could find what he needed quickly. Now all was gone.

Jefferson's mother and the children crowded into the overseer's house temporarily, and Jefferson moved to his one finished room at Monticello. Work continued on the house.

After this, his first concern was about books. He might get some from Philadelphia fairly soon; but the majority must be ordered from London—that letter should be sent now.

He went to his desk, got out paper and quill, and began his list: Shakespeare, Milton, Ovid, Vergil, Hume's History of England, English, French, Latin, Greek, and German dictionaries; the philosophers, Locke, Hobbes, Bacon, Rousseau—the sheet was full. He paused to glance back; and with that glance he suddenly realized the change that had come in his interests in recent months. Those last names revealed it.

Thomas Jefferson was now nearing twenty-seven, and ever since he had learned to read in the little white schoolhouse at Tuckahoe he had read avidly to satisfy his lively curiosity about the world. He was interested in everything—science, history, literature, law.

But since he had been a burgess, his interest in political science, the art of government, had grown steadily. As he thought of the books he must have, he saw that, for him, the most important study was man and his relation to other men. Government should not *rule;* it should be a kind of umpire, seeing that every man obeyed laws that would bring the greatest good to all.

During the last few months Jefferson had been rereading books with this new interest in mind. And he had found new and exciting books, such as the work of the French philosopher Montesquieu. He took another sheet and wrote names he might once have passed by; now he could hardly wait till the books arrived. In two years Jefferson had accumulated twelve hundred and fifty volumes.

Sometime that summer of 1770, Jefferson met Martha Wayles Skelton, a beautiful, talented, and wealthy widow. Her father was a successful lawyer; his plantation, The Forest, lay between Richmond and Williamsburg. Because of her good mind, her father had given her an excellent education, and she was a fine musician. Here, for the first time since his sister Jane's death, Thomas found a woman who could play and sing and also talk on topics that interested him. He fell in love at once.

Naturally he was not the charming Martha's only suitor. Jefferson pretended that he came to consult with Mr. Wayles, and so excused his frequent visits. But he fooled no one but himself. Why shouldn't he be interested in lovely Martha, the household whispered? Neighborhood gossips told many a romantic tale. But there was one favorite. One summer day four suitors chanced to arrive at The Forest at the same time. They reined their horses by the gate and wondered who should go in first—there would be little comfort to any if they went together.

"We'll draw for first chance," one said, and Jefferson won that right. He grinned at the others' disappointment and galloped up the drive.

In a little while, music of the harpsichord drifted from the drawing-room windows. Then the sound of singing, Martha's voice blending with Jefferson's. Impatiently, the men fidgeted, and their horses pawed the dust. Then came strains of a violin.

"That does it!" the tallest suitor exclaimed. "He's been there two hours and seems as though he is just tuning up. I'm going home!"

According to the neighbors, the three mounted and rode away, leaving the field to Jefferson.

Perhaps Thomas and Martha were engaged the summer of 1771, for that is when he wrote to England ordering a handsome harpsichord. The instrument was to be made of "solid mahogany with fine workmanship and plenty of spare strings. It must be worthy of acceptance of a lady for whom I intend it," the order said.

The wedding was New Year's Day, 1772, and the Wayles home was crowded with guests. After the great dinner and the equally important "infair" entertaining on the following days, the bride and groom left in a chaise for Monticello, nearly a hundred miles away. Probably they stopped at Tuckahoe and perhaps with other relatives on the journey, for creeks were swollen and hard to cross and snow was deep on the hills.

Night was falling—and more snow with it—when they were eight miles away from Monticello. Jefferson decided to leave the chaise at an overseer's cottage and finish the ride on horseback. But the snow was blinding; the going, hard. When they came upon a shelter at the foot of the mountain, Jefferson blanketed the horses and left them; he fastened the door against the wind, and they climbed on foot to his bachelor home. The main house was not yet finished.

Breathless but happy, they came into the dark room.

"Wait now, Martha, and I'll make a light," Jefferson said. He found a candle and flint, and lighted the fire, always ready on the hearth.

"I have some of my mother's wine, here, somewhere." He rummaged behind the books and found it.

"Hungry?" he asked, eyeing her anxiously. This was not what he had planned.

Martha shook her head and began to hum one of his favorite tunes. . . .

The next morning his bride pulled a curtain and looked out west.

"Why, Tom!" she exclaimed. "It's beautiful! Look!"

Laughing, he came and slipped his arm around her. "Had you not believed me? Did I not tell you that our mountaintop is beautiful? There, the world is at your feet, as I promised you."

In silent wonder they watched the scene spread before their eyes. Fresh snow glistened and sparkled in the sunshine. To the west, under a blue-violet haze, the peaks of the Blue Ridge Range looked cold and brilliant, tipped with snow. Below, nearby, the tiny village of Charlottesville was roofed with snow. Drifting smoke from village hearths gave life and movement to the vast stillness.

"But we can't eat a view!" Suddenly Jefferson was hungry. "Give me ten minutes, Martha. I'll let Jupiter and Sulkey know we are here—they'll do the rest."

He ran out and down the slope to the brick houses under the snow-covered terrace where the servants lived.

"Marster Tom!" Jupiter could hardly believe his eyes. "You home? We watched till dark and then gave up!"

"We got in late." Jefferson grinned like a schoolboy. "We'd dined; so we weren't hungry. I left the chaise at Blenheims and the horses in the little field house. Better fetch them first. Lucky you keep feed there; I gave them some last night. But first call Sulkey. We want breakfast."

"You'll have it!" Jupiter rang the plantation bell to tell the people that Mr. Jefferson and his lady had come home.

chapter seven

Young Men Take the Lead

THE BRIDE of Thomas Jefferson was not destined to enjoy a life of leisure. She brought to her husband houses and lands and slaves, doubling his wealth. But the welfare of all these people was the business of the plantation mistress; Mrs. Jefferson must see to it that they were properly fed, clothed, and nursed when ill.

Kindness was a tradition at Monticello, as it had been at Shadwell. Jefferson spoke of his slaves as "my people" or occasionally as servants—not as slaves. He trained them in a trade and was more inclined to use praise than censure as an incentive. They adored him. His plantations were free from the labor troubles that plagued many Southerners.

Martha Jefferson knew that her husband's methodical ways were as much a part of his nature as his love of music. So she determined to please him by keeping records. She found a discarded leather notebook and thriftily turned it upside down and began her new entries in the back. She set down yards of cloth, number of dresses, and many other details.

The next year, Martha's father died, and when the Wayles estate was settled the Jeffersons found they had a considerable inheritance, but also a debt in England. This debt was regrettable but not really a worry, as Jefferson had an excellent income. His farms brought in some two thousand dollars a year in cash besides the living, and his books showed he earned three thousand at law. Life seemed very easy and agreeable.

The Jeffersons enjoyed a stay of two months in Williamsburg during the spring of 1772. Then they returned to Monticello. Their daughter Martha was born there in the autumn.

From the time his new books began to arrive, Jefferson had set himself to study the philosophy of government. This winter of 1772-3 he was hard at it. He reread his Bible and Aristotle, the Greek philosopher of the fourth century B.C., and other works. He found that many thoughtful men had written about the rights of human beings; about the relation of men to each other and to government. He read that men were born "free" but that in a society where everyone was free, no man should take "rights" that would hurt someone else.

This sounded much like the Golden Rule, "Love thy neighbor as thyself"; but it raised questions. What is freedom? Where does liberty end? Who is to decide?

Somewhere in this study, Jefferson began to wonder about the laws of Virginia—how good were they, really? Mostly they were brought from England, royal laws often for the advantage of the king and his court. Why should a distant king make rules for a country he had not even seen? Should not laws be made by the people who must obey them? Some time, Jefferson promised himself, he would study these matters. Now the general court was about to open, and he had legal work promised. He reluctantly set out for Williamsburg.

Colonial affairs were quiet—on the surface. Governor Botetourt had died, and Lord Dunmore had been sent to Virginia to succeed him. Dunmore promptly dissolved the assembly when they did not please him; but there was no open quarrel. By contrast, troubles in New England ports were growing more serious. Samuel Adams was called a "firebrand" because he spoke up daringly for the colony.

In the early spring of 1773, a group of friends met in a small room at the Raleigh Tavern.

"We all know that events are making it necessary for us to understand what our sister colonies are thinking," Jefferson said, as he closed the door cautiously and pulled up a chair by Dabney Carr.

"We should be in touch with each other by letter," Dabney remarked. "That would be—"

"Sam Adams proposed that a year or so ago," Francis Lee interrupted. "He got a correspondence going between towns in Massachusetts, and it works well, I hear."

"They call Adams a firebrand," Patrick Henry chuckled, "but the times need fire. Virginians need arousing."

"Suppose we present a resolution asking for inter-colonial correspondence," Jefferson said. "Would it pass?"

"Depends on the presentation," Richard Henry Lee told him. "Likely you have the resolution already written, Tom. Present it yourself."

Jefferson flushed. "As a matter of fact I do have a rough draft." He smiled at Lee. "But I am no speaker. I suggest that Carr make the presentation." He turned to his brother-in-law with confidence. Others in the room, like Jefferson, had observed Carr's growing skill in court work. They approved the plan.

A few days later, Dabney Carr presented a resolution to form a committee of correspondence between the colonies. The bill passed, and a committee headed by Randolph was appointed.

As that session adjourned, members praised Carr.

"Patrick Henry himself could not have spoken better," several were heard to say. "Carr has a great future."

Dabney was grateful for his chance. He liked to speak.

But alas! The great future was not to be. In two months Dabney Carr was dead from a fever. Heartbroken, Jefferson had him buried under their favorite oak at Monticello. He little thought when they promised this for each other only fifteen years before that brilliant Dabney would die at thirty!

"My home is yours!" Thomas pledged his widowed sister. "Dabney's children are as mine." There were six young Carrs, three boys and three girls.

"Dabney had been doing well," his widow said. "We were saving, too. For the present we shall live in our little home, Tom. He would want it. Perhaps when time for education comes—" she paused, appalled at the future.

"Then I shall try to take a father's place. It's a promise, Sister," Jefferson said, much moved.

Meanwhile, after that committee of correspondence was appointed, Governor Dunmore had dissolved the assembly. Undaunted, the members met in Raleigh Tavern, and the committee got its work under way.

A year later, in 1774, the spring assembly was in session when startling news came to Virginia. The king had ordered the Port of Boston closed on June first in retaliation for the so-called "Boston Tea Party"!

"That 'tea party' was an honest protest against the tax on tea!" a burgess exclaimed angrily.

"Bostonians threw tea into the bay—that's not legal."

"The king punishes all shippers and merchants for the bold protest of a few men." Words flew so fast that voices were lost in confusion. Men pushed out into the hall, shouting.

"The king has no right—"

"It's Parliament! Don't blame the king!"

"Gentlemen! Gentlemen!" The honored voice of George Wythe quieted the tumult. "Let us not draw hasty conclusions. We need more facts. Boldness is ill-advised."

"But sir," Jefferson protested to his friend, "we must stand by Massachusetts!"

Francis Lee pulled at Jefferson's sleeve.

"Meet me in the Council Room," he whispered. "In the library there we may find a precedent that will appease Wythe and satisfy us at the same time."

When six or eight young men had gathered in the library, Patrick Henry closed the door.

"We need to find some dramatic act that will arouse the people," he said frowning as he slumped in a chair. Jefferson was at the shelves, turning book pages thoughtfully.

"A Fast Day!" he cried suddenly. "We have not had a Fast Day for twenty years. It will focus attention on this affront to colonial liberty."

"And who will propose it?" Patrick demanded sarcastically. "One of us would be hooted down. Already we are called radicals!" The young men were silent.

"I suggest Robert Carter Nicholas," said Jefferson, breaking that stillness. "He is known for his piety. His word will carry the authority we need." Nicholas was the man who had criticized Jefferson's first work in the assembly; but in the years since, resentment had faded.

Nicholas accepted the assignment, and the bill passed at

once. Clergymen all over the colony were invited to pray for peace and harmony with the mother country.

Of course Dunmore dissolved the assembly. The burgesses marched to the tavern, as before, and voted to join with other colonies in a protest to the king.

"This protest should come from a meeting of the colonies," a burgess said.

"Call it a colonial congress," another said.

"That should show the king and Parliament that an affront to one colony is an affront to us all." Men nodded agreement.

"Such a congress should meet soon."

"But its members should be specially chosen."

Many made good suggestions for setting the plan in motion. It was soon decided that each county should elect a delegate. These county men were to meet August first and choose representatives for the proposed colonial congress in September. Travel and communication difficulties would make that much time necessary. Then the meeting adjourned to carry out plans for the Fast Day.

That first day of June, 1774, was long remembered in Virginia. Churches were packed. In Williamsburg, ladies and gentlemen who came in fine coaches mingled with the humblest townsmen as all flocked to Bruton Parish Church. Clergymen prayed that the king might modify his harshness to his loyal people. Few worshipers cared about distant Boston. But they suddenly realized that the king's wrath might descend upon Virginia, too.

At the county elections, Fairfax elected George Washington; Louisa, Patrick Henry; and Albemarle, Thomas Jefferson.

The way of life in Virginia accustomed young planters to accept responsibility for the welfare of many persons; their offices as vestrymen, justices of the peace, burgesses, gave early training for public life. Delegates at that August meeting formed one of the most distinguished groups in colonial history.

Thomas Jefferson shut himself up with his books for hours each day. He pondered on the works of Greek, Roman, French, and English philosophers, trying to select from their wisdom ideas that could be fitted to American conditions and needs. By July he had summed up his thinking in an essay he called, "A Summary View of the Rights of British America."

"When we meet, we shall have to write instructions for our delegates to the Congress," he said to his wife. "I hope these thoughts will be helpful." He put two copies in his saddlebag and left for Williamsburg with Jupiter.

The weather was muggy and hot. Flies followed the chaise in clouds. Before they had gone half the journey, Jefferson was taken ill with dysentery.

"I shall have to turn back," he said to Jupiter. "Take my papers and deliver them in Williamsburg. One is for Patrick Henry; one for Peyton Randolph—"

"But Marster Tom," Jupiter began to object—

"Say nothing. Do what I tell you!" Jefferson was so ill that his tone was sharp. Jupiter got the papers from the bag and helped turn the chaise around. Then, reluctantly, he went on.

Jefferson never knew quite how he got home. He was very ill. Luckily the horse was familiar with the road.

In Williamsburg, Jupiter faithfully delivered the documents to the two men. Patrick Henry glanced at his copy and then mislaid it; he was careless about anything that must be read. Peyton Randolph began to read his copy. A startled look came to his eyes; he folded the paper carefully and said to a friend, "Come to my room this evening. I am asking some others, also. I have something from Tom Jefferson that needs thought."

That evening, behind a closed door, Randolph spread out Jefferson's paper and explained how it came to him.

"The paper is wise and thoughtful; but very bold. Tom reviews the settlement of America and reminds us that individual men, not the English government, opened up the new world. They fought for themselves; they lived under laws accepted in England. They must continue as free men."

Randolph glanced up. Men were listening intently.

"Tom points out definite injustices; we all resent it that a man cannot even make a hat from a coonskin he hunted on his own land. We must send our own iron oversea for manufacture. We make shippers rich and ourselves poor. The Stamp Act, the closing of the Port of Boston, taking away the right of trial by jury—but let me read you what he says:

" 'If the pulse of his people shall beat calmly under this experiment, another and another will be tried, until the measure of despotism be filled up.' You gentlemen must read the paper; I find it bold, perhaps too daring. Tom does not smooth over anything; 'Let those flatter who fear: it is not an American art,' he writes, 'the whole art of government consists in the art of being honest. The God who gave us life, gave us liberty at the same time.' He ends with a prayer for harmony. You should read this yourselves."

A murmur of shock, even fear, was heard. Men eyed each other uneasily. Later several agreed that the paper was interesting but much too bold. In the end, instructions of great mildness were voted for the delegates.

Word of this voting came to Jefferson, convalescing on his mountain, and he was hardly surprised.

"I proposed too long a leap for our citizens," he said to Martha quietly. "Less revolutionary ideas are familiar; the leaders should not be too far ahead."

But the writing of that Summary View was not wasted labor. Randolph had it printed; George Washington and many other Virginians read it. Later it was issued in England and made a great stir. Its author was called an "outlaw."

Thomas Jefferson was now thirty-one years old and a successful lawyer. A year earlier he had declined to accept Mr. Nicholas's practice when that gentleman wished to retire. Now, he decided to withdraw from his own profitable practice and give all his time and thought to government. He was already favorably known as lawyer, architect, botanist, musician, farmer, and somewhat of an inventor. Human beings now became his main interest—men, and their relations to each other. From

the time his Summary View was published he came to be recognized also as a writer and a statesman.

The First Continental Congress opened in Philadelphia
in September, 1774. Thomas Jefferson was not a delegate; his
suggestions for the delegates had not been adopted. But many
men had read his Summary View; its bold spirit seemed to be
present in men's minds.

When the Congress opened, Patrick Henry rose at once and
made a plea for unity.

"The distinction between Virginians, Pennsylvanians, New
Yorkers, New Englanders, is no more. I am not a Virginian;
I am an American." That use of the word was new.

A feeling of optimism hung over the meeting. Independence was not discussed. Now that colonists had joined
together, king and Parliament would be reasonable, and all
would be well. The Congress adjourned to meet in a year "if
wrongs still continued." That seemed most unlikely.

Governor Dunmore did not call a Virginia assembly in
the spring of 1775; so county delegates, elected the year before,
met in Richmond in March. Friction with England had not
ended, as men had hoped. Another session of the Continental
Congress was needed: reports must be heard and delegates
instructed. Most Virginians were annoyed but still loyal to
their king.

As delegates gathered in St. John's Church, this loyalty
began to irritate Patrick Henry. "Can't they see that the king
waits for submission, then plans more affronts?" he cried.

But the convention began agreeably, and older men tried to keep the loyal tone. A routine resolution ended with a wish that the colony return "to those halcyon days when we lived a free and happy people."

This was too much for Henry! He jumped up and demanded that the colony be placed in a state of defense. Men stared.

"I move a committee be appointed to arm and train for defense!" he shouted. Older men rose and tried to be heard above the confused babel of talk.

"What tempts us to war?"

"We are not ready! Where are stores, generals, money?"

"We must be patient. England really needs us!"

Opposition always inspired Henry. Now he rose slowly, impressive in spite of shabby clothes and a slouch. His low voice hushed the tumult. Men turned to listen as he recited colonial wrongs and demanded, "When will you be ready to fight? Next week? Next year?"

Over their rapt attention his voice challenged them. "Peace! Peace! There is no peace! Why stand we here idle? Is life so dear or peace so sweet as to be purchased at the price of chains and slavery? We must fight!

"I know not what course others may take; but as for me, give me liberty or give me death!"

In an awed silence Henry sank to his seat.

Then there was shouting and a roar of talk. His motion to put the colony in a state of defense was voted on. It passed— 65-60; close, but it was seen that the young, vigorous men passed it.

Soon the committee to arm Virginia was appointed. Its roster included Henry, Jefferson, Washington, and Richard Henry Lee. The young men of Virginia were on the march.

chapter eight

A Day to Remember

TOWARD THE END of the session in Richmond, that Virginia convention elected delegates to Congress. Peyton Randolph was continued as the leader; Washington and Henry were also re-elected. Jefferson's name was not on the list. On the last day, someone remembered the governor.

"Suppose Dunmore calls a meeting of the burgesses? That would oblige Randolph to stay in Williamsburg." Randolph was the speaker of the regular Virginia assembly as well as leader of the delegates to Congress. "We should have someone in his place."

So Thomas Jefferson was elected to the Colonial Congress —as an alternate.

Meanwhile, Governor Dunmore actually was considering a call for an assembly. Williamsburg was deserted. But he wondered whether it was better to call back rebel Virginians or let them scatter to their homes. Suddenly he thought of the powder stored in the powder house near the Green. Virginians might blow up the town! He had it moved by night to warships on the nearby river.

Virginians were angry when news of this midnight theft got around. That powder belonged to the colony, not the king.

Patrick Henry gathered a company of the colonial militia and marched toward Williamsburg. They were a motley lot. Tomahawks and rifles were standard equipment, and hunting shirts were "official" uniforms. The men were nearing Williamsburg when peacemakers from the governor met them with a generous offer of cash for the powder.

Henry accepted the purchase. Chuckling at their easy success, the men agreed to return home.

But Dunmore did not trust them. He fortified the palace and waited until Patrick Henry was on his way to Philadelphia before he ventured to call the assembly. The burgesses were needed, Dunmore claimed, to reply to an important letter from the prime minister, Lord North.

Peyton Randolph turned back at the governor's call, and

Jefferson made ready for the journey to Philadelphia. At the last minute, he decided to go by way of Williamsburg.

"I shall travel by chaise," he told his overseer. "Have Richard make ready to go with me and lead a spare horse."

"Shall you be gone long, Uncle Tom?" Peter Carr asked. Peter was nine, now, and the Carrs had come to live at Monticello. Jefferson was teaching Peter his lessons.

"A long time, I fear, Peter. But keep up with your Latin. And write to me. I shall want to know about everything."

"Good-by, Papa!" little Martha called fondly.

Jefferson picked her up and kissed her. "Be a good girl, Patsy. Don't forget me!" With her mother and an aunt named Martha, too, a nickname was convenient. "Good-by all! Write soon!"

Jefferson was welcomed at the assembly and promptly given the task of replying to Lord North. Then, with Richard, he set out on the tedious ten-day journey to Philadelphia. Arriving in the city, they got lodgings at the home of Benjamin Randolph, a cabinetmaker.

The author of "A Summary View" did not seem a stranger. Congressmen hastened to greet this tall, ruddy man of thirty-two. Someone noted that he was the next to the youngest in the Congress. Certainly he made an excellent first impression.

"That Jefferson is prompt, frank, explicit, and decisive," John Adams wrote of him. "He will be given work at once."

On the fifteenth of June this year, 1775, George Washington was elected commander in chief of colonial forces. He was

to leave at once to join the army near Cambridge, Massachusetts. Congress decided to send with him a document explaining to the troops recent political happenings. Soldiers would
fight better if they understood that Congress believed the time
for action against British injustices had come.

   Jefferson's first task in Congress was to help write this
paper. The document the committee turned out was a compromise between bolder colonials and those who continued loyal
to the king. The stirring words of the final paragraphs were
written by Thomas Jefferson.

   After Washington departed, Congress went at the tedious
business of raising and equipping an army. Even the news
about the battle of Bunker Hill did not really unite Congress;
men's ideas differed about the size and cost of the army needed.
But a compromise was worked out on this, too.

   In August, when Congress recessed, Jefferson went home.
The quiet of Monticello was a joy after the tumult of Congress
and a big city. He worked on roads and helped to lay out an
enlarged vegetable garden, with asparagus, artichokes, and several kinds of greens not commonly grown. A gardener Jefferson
brought from Italy planted a vineyard on the hillside. The
orchard was increased with nectarines, apricots, and new apple
and cherry trees. There was even time for music.

   Jefferson was about to return to Congress when the new
baby, little Jane, died. He felt he must not leave his wife immediately; his going would add heavy duties to her daily tasks.
The Carr children needed him, too. The month of September

was almost over when he finally got off to Philadelphia.

He found Congress still wrangling about army rules and expenses. He saw that they were sick of debate and of each other. For himself he was miserable as days went by and he had no word from Virginia. Was his wife ill? Had she gone to her sister's? Were they keeping bad news from him?

"The suspense is too terrible," he wrote. "If anything has happened let me know." But no letters came.

In December he went home. Each colony had but one vote; Richard Henry Lee was now leader of the Virginia delegation, and the colony would not suffer by Jefferson's absence.

He found Mrs. Jefferson very frail and decided to stay until she improved. So it happened that during those winter months, while public opinion was changing fast, Thomas Jefferson was far away, on his mountaintop.

There he had time to read and to think. He studied a pamphlet called "Common Sense," written by an Englishman, Thomas Paine, who had come to America at the suggestion of Dr. Franklin. The paper was published early in 1776, and by late spring ten thousand copies had been sold.

Paine wrote: "Government even in its best state is but a necessary evil; in its worst, an intolerable one . . . Ye that dare oppose not only tyranny, but the tyrant, stand forth!" Readers were stirred by such heady words. It was said that Washington called it "sound doctrine."

Trouble in Massachusetts had been dramatic, and Washington was there with the army. But Virginia had her dangers, too. The British had set Norfolk on fire; a slave rebellion, thought to be inspired by the British, was attempted. Planters along the rivers were harassed. John Page feared his beautiful Rosewell might be burned.

In Virginia, as in New England, the cautious mood of a few months earlier was changing to rebellion. Virginia delegates to the Third Continental Congress, meeting May, 1776, were instructed to propose that the colonies be free and independent states and that the Congress appoint a committee to write a declaration of independence and a plan for a new government.

This same spring Jefferson was still living the quiet life of a country gentleman. He stocked his woods with deer and daily took the children out to feed them. Then he went to his office, a one-room building opposite his first bachelor quarters. There he studied and wrote letters by the hour.

The stables were under the terrace leading to this office. One day as Jefferson was going to dinner, he heard strange sounds.

"What's up?" he leaned over the railing to ask.

"A new foal, Marster Tom," Richard said. "The Fearnought line will carry on."

"I'll fetch the children!" Jefferson hurried to the house.

"I have something to show you!" he said, and set little Patsy on his shoulder. "Come along!" He held the hand of Dabney, Jr., the youngest Carr. Others ran along with him to the stables.

"May I touch the baby horse, Papa?" Patsy asked.

"Yes, pat his neck." Jefferson leaned over so she could reach. "You may, too, if you are gentle," he told the Carrs. "See how fine and soft he feels. Yet he will be a great runner." The children were enchanted.

Mrs. Jefferson rejoiced in each day that her husband was at home. She improved, and he had begun to think of leaving, when his mother died. In April he was taken ill with a migraine headache, the first of many that were to plague him. But in

May the time came when he must go to Philadelphia. Bob, who had been chosen as Jefferson's body servant this time, brought the chaise around.

"I wish I were going to Williamsburg," Jefferson said, pausing by the chaise. "I distrust crowds. Real work is done by small groups—but a man must go where duty calls. We'll take the Culpepper road. The mountains will be with me longer."

"You and your mountains," his wife teased him.

"I'd like to carry them to Philadelphia," he retorted, smiling. "It is easier for a man to think straight when he can 'lift up his eyes unto the hills' each morning."

In Philadelphia Jefferson rented rooms from a bricklayer named Graff. Bob unpacked while Jefferson did errands. He had brought with him a drawing for a small writing desk which he wanted his landlord of the year before to make.

"That'll be a neat little desk." Ben Randolph was pleased to be remembered with an order. "I shall make it right away, sir. You'll be wanting it." In a few days Ben brought the writing desk, and Bob put it on the table. It was a handsome thing, though small.

In Congress, Jefferson was put on a Canadian Affairs Committee and given other duties. But he took time to draft a constitution for Virginia. He sent it south by George Wythe when Wythe left for Williamsburg.

On the seventh of June, Richard Henry Lee rose and presented to Congress a resolution which the Virginia assembly had passed and sent to Philadelphia by Lee. At first, men hardly listened; then the room was hushed in startled astonishment. Lee was reading bold words:

"The United colonies are and ought to be free and independent states . . . absolved from all allegiance to the British Crown." This from Virginia was amazing boldness. Men rose, shouting to be heard. The room was in a tumult.

Jefferson listened both to Lee's words and to the shouting. Then he whispered to a colleague, "The middle colonies and South Carolina seem not quite ready yet."

"Better delay the vote rather than risk defeat, eh, Tom?"

Someone across the room had the same thought, and a motion was passed to delay action until July first.

The room quieted, and a delegate moved to appoint a committee to prepare a declaration of independence from England. This was not quite as strong as Lee's resolution. It passed; and John Adams of Massachusetts, Roger Sherman, Connecticut, Benjamin Franklin, Pennsylvania, Robert Livingston, New York, and Thomas Jefferson, Virginia, were appointed.

"A nice choice, geographically," someone remarked.

The four who were present came together to arrange a time and place for meeting.

"Dr. Franklin is not well; suppose we meet with him," one said. "We should get at the work at once." So it was agreed that the committee would go to Franklin's house on Bristol Street. They found the statesman sitting in a big chair with his gouty foot propped on a stool. Windows were open; fragrance from his garden drifted in as the men pulled chairs around their host.

"Five is too large a group for the actual work of writing," Franklin said, after they had talked for a time. "I suggest that one man prepare a draft and then we all go at it."

"That man should be Jefferson," John Adams said quickly.

"Indeed, no!" Jefferson said, flushing. "The matter needs more competence than I possess, sir."

"John is right." Franklin ignored Jefferson's protest. "Virginia has taken the lead; a Virginian should write the paper. The middle colonies are not yet ready."

"The work will go better if New England keeps out," Adams remarked. "What with the so-called Boston Tea Party, Bunker Hill, and the writings of Sam Adams, we have the name of being dangerous radicals."

Franklin laughed—then winced with gouty pain.

"You see a British enemy behind every paper, John!"

"But I am right, believe me," Adams insisted. "A Virginian is needed for this work. Jefferson has studied and thought more on the matter than any of us." The others approved his feeling. So Jefferson went to his rooms, opened his new writing desk, sharpened a pen, and laid out paper. Then he began to write. Little Mrs. Graff, sensing important work, tried to protect him from interruptions.

"Mr. Jefferson is busy this morning, sir. Could you leave a message for him?" she would say to callers.

Bob had packed books, but Jefferson did not read. The time for learning from history was ended. Now he must shape the best thinking of past philosophers into a new creed for Americans. Why now? Because the time had come when it was necessary to separate from old ties; when men of a new world should stand alone. He dipped a pen in the inkpot, and his driving thoughts sent it speeding across the paper.

"All men are created equal," he wrote, and paused. Were the people ready for that bold statement? Would they under-

stand that the goal of political equality he stated was quite
different from physical, mental, or economic equality no gov-
erment could promise? Colonials had little education, on the
average; but he trusted them to understand. One must have
faith and make a beginning. He wrote on.

The document was days in growing. When Jefferson went
out to eat, Mrs. Graff slipped in and tidied his room, cherishing
every scrap of paper. When he did not leave, she brought him
hot soup, nourishing meat, and well cooked vegetables that he
liked. He grew pale. He would not let Bob cut his hair;
any fuss fretted him. He wanted only to think and to write.

The final words as he set them down were very simple:
"And for the support of this declaration, we mutually pledge
to each other our lives, our fortunes, and our sacred honor."
There, it was written.

On Friday, the twenty-eighth of June, the declaration was
read to the House and ordered put upon the table. On Monday,
July first, the earlier Virginia resolution—that the colonies be
declared free and independent states—was reopened, debated,
and, on the following day, passed.

Then the Declaration of Independence prepared by the
committee of five was taken up, and for two days members
of Congress argued hotly over this phrase and that. Jefferson
sat silent, flushed and miserable. By July fourth, debate had
grown acrimonious. The heat was frightful, and clouds of flies
from the livery stable next door were maddening.

Late in the day the vote was taken; the Declaration was

accepted. Jefferson sighed. Cherished sentences had been deleted; the most serious loss was the section against slavery. Perhaps men were not ready for all he had hoped to include. But in the main, the changes were minor.

Jefferson left the turmoil of Congress, and as he walked on a quiet street, phrases from the paper drifted through his mind:

"When in the course of human events it becomes necessary for one people to dissolve the political bands which have connected them with another, and to assume among the powers of the earth the separate and equal station to which the laws of nature and of nature's God entitle them, a decent respect to the opinions of mankind requires that they should declare the causes which impel them to the separation.

"We hold these truths to be self-evident: that all men are created equal; that they are endowed by their Creator with certain unalienable rights, that among these are life, liberty, and the pursuit of happiness; that to secure these rights, governments are instituted among men, deriving their just powers from the consent of the governed . . ."

Suddenly Jefferson was weary. "Perhaps the whole of it is overlong," he thought. "Perhaps those few words are the meat of it and some day the king and his power, the colonies and their wrongs, will be forgotten. Today—or so it seems to me—we have taken a step on the road toward man's freedom. Perhaps July the fourth, 1776, will be a day to remember."

Summer night was falling. A welcome breeze stirred as he turned and went to his room.

chapter nine

New Laws for Virginia

PRINTED COPIES of the Declaration of Independence were carried throughout the colonies by fast riders. The Liberty Bell was rung in the square in Philadelphia after crowds listened to the reading. General Washington had the Declaration read to the troops on Long Island.

The stirring words made clear the goal of battle and united conservatives and radical Whigs. Tories, colonists who were still loyal to the king, fled to England or to Canada if they could leave.

After the parades and the bonfires, after the ringing of bells and rejoicing, Congress resumed its business. A committee of minor statesmen was appointed to prepare Articles of Confederation—a proposed working agreement between states. There was little interest in it; the Articles read in Congress on the twelfth of July were received with indifference. Two years were to pass before they were ratified by all the states.

Jefferson was busy on several committees; one was to select a design for a seal for the new nation.

During June, when Jefferson had been writing the Declaration of Independence, Virginians had been setting up a new government for their state. George Mason wrote a Declaration of Rights—some called it the "Bill of Rights"—and it was accepted by the Virginia assembly. A fortnight later a new state constitution was adopted. These were excellent papers and became models for other states and for the nation. They provided for a house of delegates and a senate which should then elect a council and a governor. When the new bodies met, Patrick Henry was elected governor and Thomas Jefferson, a congressman.

Jefferson declined this office for two reasons; he wanted to help get the new state government started, and he felt he must work nearer home because of his wife's frail health. For the same reasons, he declined a most attractive appointment to serve with Dr. Franklin in France on a commission to make trade arrangements for the new United States.

But he did accept election to represent Albemarle County

in the Virginia assembly. He felt happy when, with Mrs. Jefferson, he set out for Williamsburg. The George Wythes were in Philadelphia and the Jeffersons were to use their house; Martha could make the journey if they went slowly.

"I feel it a good omen—to have you with me," Jefferson remarked on the way. "I do hope that at this assembly we can start making better civil laws for Virginia."

"You care about that, don't you, Tom," she said proudly.

"A new government is the whole object of the present controversy," he said. "We must work fast while the people are thinking about political evils. Their mood may not last."

Soon they were settled in the Wythe house, and Jefferson went to the opening of the assembly. After that, people often noticed this tall vigorous man who strode along the Green each morning and turned to the capitol. But few guessed that the thoughts under his bushy red hair were about government for a free state and nation. They did not know that he had been studying for years—and now the time for action had come.

Thomas Jefferson had ideas about what was needed. While other men were fighting for freedom, he was looking beyond victory, hoping to have laws ready so that freedom gained by the war could be turned to good use and made safe.

First he wanted to keep the country from rule by a *few*. He believed in men; he wanted more voters in his state. Virginia, and indeed the whole nation, needed men who owned small farms and were willing to work. Laws must be changed so that the great estates were divided.

Second, men must be sure of bodily safety; they must not be slaves, or be punished cruelly for trifling crimes.

Third, education must be free. Only educated men could vote wisely, Jefferson thought.

Fourth, men must be allowed to worship God, each in his own way. There must be no state church.

Such vital changes would never come quickly. But Jefferson believed that if Virginia made new laws, freeing men's land, bodies, minds, and souls, it would be a start.

Ever since Dunmore left Virginia, the courts of law had been closed. So Jefferson's first move was to have new courts opened. Then he proposed a bill to change some laws of inheritance, and another bill to order a study of all Virginia's laws with the idea of making better ones. Under his vigorous leadership these bills passed.

The assembly appointed a committee of five to do the work of revision—Jefferson, Wythe, Mason, Edmund Pendleton, and Thomas L. Lee. They decided to meet in Fredericksburg later and plan the project.

Bright autumn colors faded. Boxwood hedges were dark green when the assembly ended and the Jeffersons went home.

There, newspapers and letters brought word of the war. Patriots were having a hard time. The Continental Congress was wrangling over army supplies, and the soldiers were cold and hungry at Valley Forge.

War brought serious money troubles, too. Thousands suffered from inflation—Jefferson with the rest. He had sold land to pay his father-in-law's debts; he had put the amount in trust to be sent to England. Now, because of the war, the notes were returned to him. The whole sum, more than $13,000, would now buy only one overcoat. He needed the coat; so he bought it. He must sell more land to pay the debt.

Some men paid debts in worthless paper money printed in quantities by various states. Washington lost heavily from such slick practice. There was profiteering in army supplies that shocked honest men.

"The avarice of individuals will be more fatal to the liberties of America than the sword of the enemy," a friend in Congress wrote to Jefferson.

This winter Thomas Paine published a paper called *The Crisis* in which he said, "These are the times that try men's souls." People had faith in George Washington and believed that somehow he would save them. Thomas Jefferson was hardly noticed. War was more dramatic than making laws to guard the freedom the war hoped to win.

But Jefferson did not seem disheartened that January of 1777 when he drove to Fredericksburg to begin his study of Virginia's outmoded laws. His faith in men and in human progress toward a free and better government was firm.

The committee of five men appointed by the Virginia assembly gathered around a table to plan their important task.

"Our work, as I see it," Pendleton began briskly, "is to make a new code of law. Start fresh."

"I cannot write laws," Lee protested. "I am not a lawyer."

"Nor am I," Mason said. "Do we need *new* laws?"

"As I see it, no," Jefferson told him. "Virginia's laws, good and bad, have been tested in the courts. People are used to them. I favor a study of the entire legal code. Then we can drop bad laws and simplify others."

"You made a good beginning when entail was abolished with hardly a ripple," Mason remarked, referring to the change in those laws of inheritance that were altered so easily in the fall.

"Now we can go at primogeniture," Jefferson said. These two legal terms were familiar to Virginians then but later fell into disuse. Entailed land was restricted from ordinary laws of inheritance. By entail, huge land grants from the king could continue to be held by one man. The law of primogeniture gave the whole estate to the oldest son; younger sons and the daughters got nothing.

"You cannot touch primogeniture!" Pendleton exclaimed.

"We have to touch it," Jefferson said firmly. "We have to abolish it, to break up the great plantations, if we are to create a broad base of citizenship." He felt sure that a free government was safe only when controlled by a wide range of voters.

"Huge estates create a privileged class," Mason said.

"We need small farms," Lee added, "not great plantations."

"At very least we should allow the oldest son twice as much as the others," Pendleton insisted.

"Are you ready to prove that he works twice as hard and wears and eats twice as much as the others?" Jefferson asked pleasantly. "If so, we might consider it." Pendleton subsided.

After more discussion, Mason and Lee insisted that this work should be done by lawyers. They withdrew. Wythe, Pendleton, and Jefferson divided all the laws of Virginia from colonial times to that day; each agreed to study his portion and recommend changes. This work might take months. (It did require more than two years.) As it could be done at home, the meeting ended, to convene again when reports were ready.

Back at Monticello, Jefferson set himself a daily program of work as rigorous as in his student days. Hours of study and writing in his office or library; hours to attend to farms, teach Peter Carr, share music with his wife and games with

the children. They were living in the part of the main mansion that was finished. Work on the place continued for a long time.

In May, the son he longed for was born, and Jefferson was radiantly happy. But the baby died a fortnight later—his only son. Of their three children, only Patsy, now four and a half, was living. Her father was glad for hard work that helped him forget his sorrow.

One of Jefferson's many hobbies had been collecting old laws. He found them in pamphlets, books, and newspapers. Now he spread these out and studied each one, sifting the good from the bad for his report. He knew there were many legal problems.

Slavery must be abolished. About two hundred thousand Virginians were slaves—half the population. He favored training and educating them and having them work as free men. That would not break up the economy. Another phase of bodily freedom was legal punishment. He thought that only treason and murder should be punished by death.

The plan of education Jefferson worked out was to be for everyone. If parents were able to, they should pay; if not, school was to be free. Primary schools should be conveniently near—one for about every hundred children.

"We might call them 'Hundred Schools,'" he told his wife as they talked of this. "People like a name. All children should go for three years." This was a new idea in his time.

After three years, children with good minds should have more education—free, if parents could not pay. And finally the most intelligent, perhaps ten out of each hundred, should go to college. He planned also for free libraries, to provide books for all who wished to read. This was a bold and original thought then.

Perhaps the idea nearest to his heart was the law he wrote and hoped would pass freeing men from a state religion. In Virginia the state church was the Church of England. People of other creeds were called "dissenters." In the Piedmont area there were many dissenters—Quakers, Presbyterians, and others. Custom was gradually changing; dissenters could attend other churches, but they still had to pay for the state church as well as their own.

"It is good that people are not all of one sect," Jefferson said, as he walked on the terrace. "God has made us different. Each man varies in face and stature—why should all worship the same? Differences make people think." This tolerance of the opinions of others was very rare at this time.

As Jefferson worked on all the laws, he often jotted down thoughts about religion; it was important to him.

"The care of every man's soul belongs to himself. What if he neglect it? Well, what if he neglect the care of his health, or his estate? Will the magistrate make a law that he shall not be sick or poor? Laws provide for injury from others but not from ourselves. God himself will not save men against their wills.

"Religion is a personal thing: one cannot be compelled to believe. I may grow rich by an art I am compelled to follow, I may recover health by medicine I am compelled to take; but I cannot be saved by a worship I disbelieve."

Sometimes when Jefferson worked long, he heard a soft knock at the office door. Listening, he laid down his pen.

"Yes?" he asked, with a pleased smile.

"Papa, isn't it time to feed the deer?" Patsy peeked in the door to say. "I have a treat for the baby fawn."

He tossed her onto his shoulder, and off they went to the woods.

On an August morning in 1778, her father came to Patsy as she was playing near the west door.

"Want to see something?" he asked mysteriously.

"Will I like it?" she demanded. "Where is it?"

"I like it," he grinned at her. " It's in your mother's room. Come and see." He held out a hand, and Patsy ran to him.

"There, what do you think of that? A baby sister!" Mrs. Jefferson turned down the blanket so Patsy could see. "Her name is Mary. And some day you may play with her."

"I think she looks like you, my dear," Jefferson said to his wife, pleased with his discovery. "We must take care of them, Patsy."

The baby needed care; but after a few weeks she thrived, and her mother grew stronger, too. It was a happy time.

In February of 1779, Wythe, Pendleton, and Jefferson met in Williamsburg. They studied each other's work sentence by sentence. They had reduced the vast jumble of archaic laws to one hundred and twenty-six, all straightforward and clear. The committee presented these to the legislature that June.

But the lawmakers were not interested. Not even the urging of the committee could prod them to action.

"They think of nothing but the war," Wythe said, discouraged.

"Naturally, for the war must be won," Jefferson answered. "We must be content with making this start. The laws are written; some day they will pass." Jefferson understood people. He was a philosopher as well as a social reformer.

His bill for religious freedom was hotly debated year after year. Considerably modified, it finally passed in 1786. Other bills were not even printed so they could be studied, until 1784. In the assemblies of 1785 and 1786, fifty-six of the hundred and twenty-six bills were passed. People are slow to vote social changes; Jefferson was wise in saying that "a start should be made."

chapter ten

Governor Jefferson

IN MANY WAYS that period in the late seventeen-seventies, when Jefferson was working on new laws, was the happiest of his life. His house was not yet finished; but he liked working on it and seeing it grow. He enjoyed riding over his farms and tramping on his hills.

The loss of two children was sad; but he had Patsy and baby Mary, and with six Carr children Monticello was brimming with young life. Patsy was having lessons with the Carr children.

Mrs. Jefferson thrived when he was at home; her duties were lightened, then, too. After her daily tasks of overseeing spinning, weaving, sewing, and housekeeping were done, she played on the harpsichord for her husband as in their courtship days. A Mr. Alberti, a musician, came up from Williamsburg; and they both took lessons from him.

Visitors came to the little mountain and stayed for days in the easy Virginia fashion. Mrs. Jefferson did not have strength for balls and formal entertaining, but friends were always welcome and were somehow tucked in the already crowded house. Some new neighbors were interesting friends.

Early in 1779, about four thousand English and German prisoners of war were marched to Albemarle County, away from war areas. They were housed in crude barracks near Charlottesville. The men were skillful and industrious; they finished those barracks, landscaped the grounds, and grew vegetables. Jefferson admired all this; and when he found that some were musicians, he invited them to Monticello.

"I hear you are making friends with the enemy," a man in town criticized.

"The cause which divides our countries cannot be settled by personal enmity," Jefferson reminded him mildly.

"Well, they do seem nice enough," the man conceded.

Jefferson reluctantly left this pleasant scene to meet with the committee on the new laws and to attend the assembly. There he heard reports of his Albemarle neighbor, George Rogers Clark, and his most recent expedition in the west.

Washington and Jefferson, more than others of their time, had a vision of the wilderness part of Virginia, that vast area which became known as the Northwest Territory. They had worked together in sponsoring Clark; reports of his dangers and successes fascinated Jefferson.

In May of 1779, Patrick Henry's third one-year term as governor of Virginia was nearing its end, and he was not eligible for another term. Liberal voters put up Jefferson; conservatives nominated John Page. Many planters were already frightened by Jefferson's proposed new laws; they worked hard to defeat him.

Candidates did not electioneer, but the vigorous work of their friends embarrassed the two men, though they did not let it disturb their long friendship. Jefferson was elected by a small margin, and Page congratulated him. Both knew that being governor was a chore; the assembly had stripped the post of most of its usefulness.

The day after he was elected—June 4, 1779—Jefferson dressed with unusual care. Richard had fetched a freshly powdered wig from the wigmaker, in honor of the occasion. The new governor wore a satin coat and silver knee buckles.

"A pity Mis' Jefferson's not here," Richard said sadly. "Is it so, there's no parade? No bonfires?"

"She and Patsy will come later," Jefferson said. "Of course there is no parade. This is a republican state. I am merely the servant of the people." Richard sighed.

Through town gossip, the servant heard later that Jefferson

had acquitted himself well. Tidewater men were elegantly dressed for the occasion; upland delegates wore their usual leggings and hunting shirts.

Ten years had gone by since Thomas Jefferson, a lawyer of twenty-six, had entered this chamber as a burgess. Now he was pledging his faith as a governor. He thanked the legislators in brief, simple words, and they congratulated him.

The new governor received many letters. Washington wrote good wishes; James Madison was "pleased to see a philosopher in public office." James Monroe, a youth of twenty-one, heard his uncle say, "Jefferson is a proper man for office."

Governer Jefferson kept bachelor quarters in the palace through the summer. In late September Mrs. Jefferson and the two daughters came to be with him. He met their carriage at the gate and led Patsy past the pansy beds, gay with fall bloom, into the mansion.

"You must feel strange, Tom," Mrs. Jefferson said, "to live in this house that was so exciting to enter when you were a student. I had not thought of that until now."

"Much has changed since Governor Fauquier lived here," Jefferson said, with a hint of regret in his voice. "He was a very elegant gentleman, Patsy. Handsome portraits of the king and queen hung on the wall there. It looks bare to me, now."

"I suppose Governor Dunmore took the pictures," Mrs. Jefferson said. "Poor man! He was so afraid of Virginians! Patsy, he made a fort out of this lovely place."

"Patrick Henry's big family made a shambles of what

Dunmore left," Jefferson added ruefully. "We have done our best at cleaning, but I have not been able to refurnish. The governor's salary *sounds* good, but it does not even buy necessities. We shall have to be very careful. But come with me, Patsy," he said cheerfully; "we'll go upstairs and see your room." Patsy clung to his hand, and they climbed the handsome carved stairway.

Despite the congratulations and the joy in his family, Jefferson knew that a storm was brewing. Actually the timing of his election could hardly have been worse for him.

The state treasury was empty. Paper money, printed by the state, had less and less value. A chicken cost ten dollars; a pound of tea, eighteen. In the usual way of governments, the assembly levied higher taxes, which the people were too poor to pay. In some places the tax collectors were mobbed by desperate, angry citizens.

Patrick Henry wrote from his home in the mountains. "I have feared that our body politic was dangerously sick. Increase of prices is a kind of habit fostered by mistaken avarice. This, more than British arms, makes me fearful of final success." He wondered whether people with "so little virtue and public spirit" deserved a free government.

A changed state of war added to financial troubles. The alliance with France had given most Americans a sense of security that was quite false. The war was far from won. Now the British army moved south in an active campaign, and for the first time Virginians felt the terror of battle at their very doors.

Virginia, under the loyal leadership of Patrick Henry and Thomas Jefferson, had supported Washington with men and arms. Now, when her own land was invaded, she had only volunteer militia—men with no training, no arms, no boats. So many horses had been sent to General Washington that farmers could not work all their fields. That summer of 1779 a blight ruined crops; hardly enough grain was harvested for the next year's seed. How was Virginia to feed the hundreds of war prisoners sent south? That was only one of the staggering problems.

The geography of Virginia and its vast size made dangers that were not understood in New England, perhaps not even by many Virginians. Long, wide rivers with countless inlets could not possibly be protected. The British could easily have taken Williamsburg had they guessed its helplessness.

In the vast, sparsely settled wilderness beyond the Piedmont, Indians, armed with British guns, slaughtered settlers with savage cruelty. No wonder men hesitated to enlist in the militia and leave their women and children at the mercy of savages!

Earlier Virginians had turned to the king for help. He had proved only feeble aid, but at least he was a "head of state" to whom they could appeal. Now they turned in despair to the new governor, Thomas Jefferson. Would his free government work now? They saw no evidence that it did.

"Why doesn't Jefferson *do* something?" frightened people cried.

They forgot, or perhaps most of them did not even know, that under Virginia's new constitution the governor merely presided over the council and saw to it that orders were carried out. He had no powers for an emergency even if he had wished to assume power—which he certainly did not.

Jefferson did use all his influence to get the capital moved to Richmond. There more legislators from the west could attend sessions—an important gain, he thought—and the government would be safer from the British. As soon as the change was approved, he moved his family into a modest rented house in the little village on the James River.

The legislators talked about erecting state buildings on Shockoe Hill, one of several hills nearby. In spite of war anxieties, Jefferson enjoyed this project. He had a new idea for three buildings, one each for the judicial, legislative, and executive branches of the government. This would illustrate to citizens the threefold government he hoped the United States would have. He drew handsome sketches. But of course nothing was done. The state had no money.

In May of 1780, Charleston, South Carolina, fell; and the British turned their full force on Virginia. From then until October of 1781, there was not a day of peace or safety in the state. Intelligence was shockingly poor. State officials never had an idea where the next blow might strike.

In December of 1780, word came to Richmond that a British fleet had been seen entering Chesapeake Bay. The governor sent an alert to the militia. Of course he had no idea of the fleet's objective. After New Year's Day he heard that it had turned up the James River.

The assemblymen hastily left Richmond. Governor Jefferson conferred with General Steuben, who was in charge of American troops in Virginia. Before long the general had more news.

"A messenger has just brought word that twenty-three British ships are bringing in hundreds of armed troops," Steuben said. "The traitor, Benedict Arnold, leads them, and they plan to take the capital."

"This shabby village!" Jefferson could not believe it.

"Richmond is the capital of Virginia," Steuben replied. "We must move public papers to safety at once."

In the darkness volunteers moved documents and supplies. Jefferson worked with them till midnight; then he rode to Tuckahoe, where he had taken his family.

Arrived there he wakened the household with loud knocking. Maids, stableboys, and the family gathered hastily in the hall.

"We must leave here at once!" he cried.

"Leave?" exclaimed Mrs. Jefferson. "Where shall we go?"

"Further up the river." He told her the bad news.

Patsy, her eyes wide and startled, peered over the bannisters. "Are the soldiers here, Papa?"

"Not now, Daughter," Jefferson answered, quietly. "Tell Sulkey to wrap you in a warm cloak—do not wait to dress. Mary, too. Make yourself and the baby warm, my dear," he added to his wife. "The night is bitter cold." The baby was little Lucy, only a few weeks old.

In five minutes they were off, driving fast. As soon as Jefferson saw them safe inside a friend's home up the river, he forded and rode back toward Richmond to help save other property.

In sight of the capital, his horse fell dead of exhaustion. Jefferson took off the saddle, staggered to a farm house, and begged a mount. The farmer lent him a colt, the only animal he had. The governor was opposite Richmond when the British entered and set fire to the city. Wooden buildings flamed, a funeral pyre of dead hopes.

Virginians blamed the governor for their tragedy.

"It was his business to protect us!" people said bitterly.

Those smoking ruins marked the lowest point in Jefferson's political career. He had had vast influence in Virginia affairs. He was esteemed as author of the Declaration of Independence and as an able lawyer who was reforming the state's ancient laws. He had served on important committees in the assembly and was known as a man who cared for the needs of the common man rather than the rich.

Suddenly that well-deserved esteem seemed forgotten because he could not keep the British out of Virginia—could not because the state had already given so much to the Revolutionary War.

And dangers steadily increased.

That spring of 1781, Lord Cornwallis and his army invaded Virginia. He crossed the state almost without opposition and was within fifty miles of Charlottesville when spies reported that the legislature was in session there—and that Governor Jefferson and his family were at Monticello.

"Call Colonel Tarleton!" Cornwallis ordered. To this fearless officer, known as the "Hunting Leopard," Cornwallis gave orders for a cross-country dash to capture state officials. Tarleton gathered his men; they set out toward Charlottesville.

Now it chanced that a young American, Captain John Jouett, was in Louisa County on a secret mission when darkness overtook him. Having ridden far, he got a bed in a small inn forty-five miles from Monticello and quickly went to sleep.

In the night he wakened and sat up, listening, warned by some keen instinct that something was amiss.

"Horses!" he told himself. "Many horses! This means trouble." He crept to the window and opened the shutter a crack. A full moon shone down on a long line of horsemen— British, traveling west! "Now what could they be after? Charlottesville is the only town west." Then he knew. "The governor! The delegates! I must get there first!"

Jouett grabbed his boots and crept stealthily down the stairs. He threw on the saddle, whispering to his horse softly as swift fingers made fast the buckles.

"We've a hard ride ahead, Prince Charley," he said softly. Prince Charley flicked an ear, and his nose quivered. "If we make it, we may save a state." Jouett led the horse out and mounted.

Horse and rider moved slowly until they were away from the village. The British were already far ahead; Jouett followed some distance behind. Then he suddenly left the road and disappeared into thick brush. Tarleton and his men would surely keep to the main highway; even that would give them plenty of trouble. Jouett and Prince Charley were on a dangerous mountain trail that only a native could know about and use. Could they beat the British?

For five grueling hours Prince Charley raced against time and those troopers. After a last dash up the winding road, Jouett stopped with a splatter of pebbles before the east entrance of Monticello. Not a sound broke the quiet. They were in time!

Jefferson had heard the flying hoofs. He threw on a dressing gown and met Jouett at the steps. Prince Charley's sides were heaving; blood flicked from dilated nostrils. Jouett was off and at the steps.

"You must leave at once, sir!" he said to the governor. "You and your lady and your children. The British are coming!"

"The *British!*" Jefferson exclaimed, astonished. "Why should they want *me?*"

"Why?" Jouett couldn't believe his ears. "You are the governor, sir. It would be a feather in their cap to take you and the delegates prisoners."

"But here! This is backwoods, Captain."

"I tell you, sir, they will soon be here!"

"Then you must warn the delegates," Jefferson said. "Come, I'll get some wine to refresh you. You have three miles yet to go."

"But you will leave at once, sir?"

Jefferson promised. Jouett gulped the wine and was off.

His flapping dressing gown made Jefferson feel very foolish as he went to waken his household. Servants made a quick breakfast. No one was frightened. The idea of being taken prisoner at Monticello was just too ridiculous.

The delegates in Charlottesville felt different. Wakened by Jouett, they gathered a quorum and voted to move the capital to Staunton, thirty-five miles west. Then they lost no time getting there.

At Monticello the carriage was brought around. The children and Mrs. Jefferson, who was ill, were sent to the home of a friend six miles away.

"You'll follow at once, Tom," Mrs. Jefferson begged.

"As soon as I gather my papers, my dear." The sun was rising as he turned to the house. Martin and Caesar were burying family silver in the cellar. "We do have use for a cellar," he remarked. "I'd wondered."

Pulling out a small spyglass, Jefferson looked toward Charlottesville. "Quiet as a Sunday. No need for such hurry." At that moment one of the field hands ran up with a warning. "They're here, sir! After you!"

Martin slammed the trap door on Caesar and the silver. Jefferson mounted his horse and was off, down the back road, as the British rode around the house.

Tarleton had orders to do no damage, but the troops made themselves quite at home. Poor Caesar was in that cellar till they left the next day. Later the British under Cornwallis went to Jefferson's Elk Hill plantation and wantonly ruined the place and stole slaves, who later died of smallpox. But Virginians had no sympathy for the governor; he should not let such things happen.

"Jefferson's kind of government is no good in wartime."

"We need someone to take hold!" people cried. "A dictator would tell us what to do!"

Jefferson could never be a dictator. But through the terrible weeks after Arnold's raid and the burning of Richmond he seemed to change from the philosopher who could wait patiently on the will of the people to a man who meant to win the war. He learned to snap out orders; to gather information for the army; to do anything that needed to be done. He determined to arrest the traitor Arnold, and sent a daring plan for his capture to George Rogers Clark. But Arnold escaped the state before Clark got the message.

The raids into Virginia continued. Lafayette, with some seven thousand troops, came to aid the state. But the well-equipped British got word, and he had to retreat to Fredericksburg.

Those were indeed hard days for Virginia.

chapter eleven

Patsy Becomes a Traveler

THAT SPRING OF 1781 was a difficult time for American patriots. General Washington was watching Clinton in New York, and the French general, Rochambeau, was at Newport. They did not dare leave those posts, though it was plain that the British had moved into the South.

General Greene was having some success in the Carolinas. General Wayne had come to support Lafayette, and they had returned to the area between Richmond and Yorktown.

Virginians were in constant danger. People on plantations and in villages lived in terror and scurried from one place to another with every fresh assault, every new rumor. The palace at Williamsburg was a hospital.

The assembly was due to meet in Charlottesville on June second to elect a council and governor. But the British had invaded Albemarle County, and the place was in chaos. That election was twice postponed, the place of meeting twice moved. Jefferson's successor was not elected until June the twelfth.

Immediately after the new governor, Thomas Nelson, Jr., took his place, the assembly passed a resolution ordering "inquiry into the conduct of the Executive of this state for the last twelve months."

Jefferson was stunned. At the moment he did not realize that the phrase meant an investigation of the council as well as of the governor. He felt it was aimed directly at him.

Albemarle County had elected Jefferson a member of the Virginia assembly. He had planned to retire; but now, his record questioned, he was grateful for the chance to defend himself. At least his neighbors had trusted him.

During that summer of 1781, the war picture changed. General Greene maneuvered Cornwallis toward Yorktown; and there, in October, the last great battle of the Revolutionary War was won.

If Jefferson's term as governor had happened to last through that month, he would have shared the triumph. He might even have been called proudly, "our War Governor."

For victory quickly changed the public mood. The investigation seemed to be forgotten. When the assembly met, Jefferson was elected a representative to Congress.

But Jefferson was a proud man. He would not allow those charges to drop. The delegates to the assembly should be made to realize the empty state treasury; the difficulty of defending a vast river waterline; the support given to General Washington all the years of the war, depleting the state's resources.

These records were in his hand when Jefferson rose and challenged the assembly to hear his case. They listened and, when he finished, wildly applauded. A resolution of trust was passed, and the charge was pronounced groundless.

The ex-governor appreciated this vindication, but the episode rankled. He declined to serve in Congress, and went to Monticello determined to live henceforth as a country gentleman.

"I am through with public service," he promised his wife. "You have taxed your strength too much; I shall stay at home."

Knowing him, Martha did not quite believe; but she loved their happy days together. Patsy and little Mary (they were calling her Polly now) were well. The baby had died; the excitement and exposure of invasions were too much for a frail infant.

About this time—1781 and 1782—several Italians settled in Albemarle County, attracted there by Jefferson's friend, Dr. Mazzei. The Jeffersons welcomed these new neighbors and entertained them. This was unusual, for Virginian hospitality did not often include southern Europeans.

While in college and studying law, Jefferson had planned to travel in Europe; but he had never found the right time for such a journey. Now Europe was coming to him. The German prisoners of war and these Italian neighbors fascinated him. He talked their language; learned about their governments and farming, their flora and fauna, and their ways of living. His alert mind welcomed this chance to learn about and to enjoy new people.

One day, after dinner, the men walked on the terrace at Monticello, and their host pointed out Monroe's home.

"You will find other agreeable neighbors," he said. "You should feel at home here. You will know what to plant, for Italy's climate is like our own, I hear."

"You would like the fruits of Italy here?" one guest asked. He had been amazed to hear his host speak Italian. He was still more surprised to see that he knew Italian plants.

"Indeed yes," Jefferson said warmly. "We should grow olive trees and mulberries for silkworms and grapes . . . "

"You like our architecture, too," another guest remarked. They had come to the end of the terrace and now turned to look back at the house. Its pleasing design and white pillars, the sunset-gleam on many windows, made an unusual picture. "Not even in Italy do we often see such beauty."

"Nor in America, either," Jefferson added, pleased with the compliment. "We are a new country. Our people have had to be concerned with building for shelter rather than beauty. But the war is ended. We can begin to enjoy the finer things."

About this time Jefferson recalled some correspondence that he had laid aside. A neighbor, Joseph Jones, member of Congress, had sent him a questionnaire which the French minister to America wanted answered. Now he read these papers.

"This is exactly the kind of work I enjoy," Jefferson said to his wife. "I shall get at this at once."

"It is quite a long list," Martha said, glancing at the papers. "Will answering take you from home?"

"Probably not. Those notebooks you tease me about are packed with information about Virginia. I shall use those."

The French minister wanted to know about the history, government, botany, geology, and crops of Virginia; about the people, their economics, religion, and social habits. At this time Europeans were very curious about the new nation.

Jefferson worked two or three hours each day; and as the work grew it became essays on churches, flora and fauna, and many other topics about Virginia. In the midst of the work his right hand was injured when he was thrown from a horse; but he taught himself to use his left hand for writing.

Sometimes he read sentences aloud to Martha and his sister and to James Madison and James Monroe when they came over. These sentences about government pleased his audience:

"The time to guard against corruption and tyranny is before they shall have gotten hold of us. It is better to keep a wolf out of the fold than to trust to drawing his teeth and claws after he shall have entered.

"Every government degenerates when trusted to the rulers.

Influence over government must be shared by the people."

Jefferson wrote plain words against war of aggression, then added: "Wars must sometimes be our lot; the wise will avoid that half of them which are produced by our own follies and injustice; and make for the other half the best preparation we can."

As this and other work went on at Monticello, Jefferson enjoyed the changing seasons. Redbud trees began to glow; dainty pink and white dogwood blooms seemed to spill over the mountains. The Blue Ridge was lavender at sunset. Pansies and narcissus bloomed in the west gardens.

In April Lucy Elizabeth was born, and the children were delighted with the new baby. But their father was troubled; the mother did not regain her strength, and soon Jefferson realized that she was dying.

Mrs. Jefferson's sister Elizabeth, Mrs. Eppes, came to help Jefferson and his sister with the nursing. Patsy and Polly called these devoted aunts Aunt Eppes and Aunt Carr in the fashion of the day. Jefferson himself stayed in his wife's room or his library next to it, treasuring every moment that he could be with her. When his Martha died, he was in a strange faint for days.

It was little Patsy who finally roused him. She kneeled by his bed and talked to him softly about the out-of-doors.

"The trees are beautiful today, Papa. The maples are red and gold. The woods flowers are almost gone, and I have not seen them. I am not allowed to ride in the woods without you.

Jupiter has our horses at the door—will you ride with me, Papa?" She paused hopefully, but he did not reply.

"I think the deer miss us, Papa. We have not fed them for many weeks." She talked on softly.

Presently he turned and took her hand. With her help he got up, and they went to the door. Jupiter almost lifted him onto his horse and followed after them. Each day after that they rode, and slowly Jefferson's interest in life was renewed. Patsy succeeded where grownups had failed.

People came to call; Jefferson was not ready for that. He took his papers on Virginia and went to one of his small plantations for a few days of hard mental work. That helped him.

When he returned to Monticello, an epidemic of smallpox was raging in the country. Jefferson packed the children into a coach and drove to Richmond. There his good friend, Dr. Archibald Cary, inoculated them. This was a serious risk then, but Jefferson nursed them safely through the danger.

While he was in Richmond friends tried to arouse his interest in current affairs.

"We need you in the federal government, Tom," one said, but Jefferson waved the idea away.

"Jemmy Madison thinks you should be the one to help Franklin negotiate the peace treaty," another said. "You would be a help in France. Few Americans speak the language."

They saw that this idea appealed to him. Messengers took this word to Congress, and soon the appointment came.

Jefferson carried the letter to his sister.

"I think I shall accept this," he said. "The journey will be a change; this says that my country needs me."

"I am glad for you, Tom; and you must not be anxious about the children. I can manage well."

"Oh, I shall not leave them for you!" Already he had thought of that. "Elizabeth has often asked for them. I shall take Polly and Lucy to her, and Patsy will go with me. I shall put her in school in Philadelphia."

Plans worked out well, and before the winter set in, Patsy and her father climbed into the chaise. Family and servants gathered at the east driveway to see them off.

"Good-by!" "Good voyage, Tom!" "Good-by, Patsy!"

Handkerchiefs were waved and shouts followed them down the mountain. The future seemed very thrilling.

In Philadelphia Jefferson found lodgings and tutors for Patsy; then disappointments began.

The winter was the coldest in the memory of man; ships were frozen tight in the ice. Jefferson's papers failed to arrive. Finally word came that the treaty was completed. Congress thanked him for his readiness to undertake a service. Nothing was said about the months of worrisome waiting and the heavy expense.

With Patsy, he left the city at once; they were on their way April 13, 1783—Jefferson's fortieth birthday. Patsy, going on eleven, was a good traveling companion. She chattered about happenings in the city or passing scenes, or kept silent. She had a gift for knowing his mood.

They went by way of Richmond and stopped there a few days. Jefferson was interested in some bills before the assembly and wanted to use his influence for their passing. It was mid-May, and the countryside was fragrant with locust blooms when the family was reunited at Monticello.

Sister Anna Jefferson, one of the twins, spent the summer there. She was a simple person, not as yet married, and she enjoyed being with her older brother. She liked to watch him going about, busy from morning until night.

Anna saw that he always wanted a project to work on. Now a bit at loose ends, he thought about his library. He had been accumulating books since the loss by fire thirteen years earlier. But he had never arranged them, nor listed them properly. This summer of 1783 he classified and catalogued the whole collection, twenty-six hundred and forty volumes, and arranged them according to subjects.

Often Jupiter or some other servant came to the door to see if Jefferson needed help. No, he liked to do it himself.

"That man," Jupiter said one day as he turned away. "You ask him anything, *anything,* and he can open a book and answer."

In June word came that the Virginia assembly had again elected Jefferson their delegate to the Continental Congress. This time, he accepted. He expected that it would be in Philadelphia; Patsy could be with him and he would be glad to serve.

Again Patsy and her father made ready to leave home. They drove a two-horse phaeton this time, and Bob rode behind leading a spare horse. That mid-October day was chilly, and a heavy frost was white on the hills as they drove away. Patsy was learning to be quite a traveler.

Arriving in Philadelphia a fortnight later, Jefferson looked up friends, found a widow with whom Patsy could live, and arranged for lessons. This was all done quickly, for Congress was to convene on November the fourth.

To his surprise, the opening session was brief. Congress adjourned to meet on the twenty-sixth at Annapolis.

Jefferson used that time to get his violin mended and to buy some new chessmen and many books. He wanted these with him at Annapolis. There was further delay in opening, as no quorum arrived until mid-December. Jefferson made some architectural drawings, read a good deal, and rode daily. He paid to have Bob taught the barbering trade. And, with James Monroe, he rented a house and set up housekeeping. They had tried lodgings and did not like them.

Though he was always busy, Jefferson missed Patsy; and he wrote long letters to her, with pages of advice on lessons, on daily planning of her time, and on behavior.

"If you are about to say anything amiss, or do anything wrong, consider beforehand; you will feel something within you which will tell you it is wrong. This is your conscience, and be sure and obey it. Our maker has given us all this faithful internal monitor."

And in another letter:

"At all times let your clothes be neat, whole, and properly put on. Be you, from the minute you rise till you go to bed, as cleanly and properly dressed as at dinner or tea."

Later a letter said:

"I am anxious to know what books you read, what tunes you play, and to receive specimens of your drawing."

Patsy wrote to him and to her aunts. She must have been lonely many times. But she loved him and knew he had done his best to put her where she could get an education. No complaint of hers would add to his problems.

Late in December, General Washington came to Annapolis to make formal end of his war service. Jefferson was chairman of the committee on arrangements for the dinner and festivities. The brilliant ceremonies lasted for two days.

But afterwards Jefferson was concerned about his country. States were careless about sending representatives. Often work of the Congress was delayed for days for lack of a quorum. The peace treaty was not even ratified as yet—and wasn't until May. Of that Congress Jefferson remarked:

"Our body was little numerous but very contentious."

Jefferson, and a few others, worked tirelessly on legislation. He drafted thirty-one papers, among which was the Ordinance of 1784—a bill to provide government for the vast new territory called the Northwest, which was then ceded to the United States. By this ordinance new territories were eventually to be admitted on equal status with the original states, and slavery was not to be allowed after 1800.

This was only a temporary measure, for protection until lands had been purchased from Indians and put up for sale to the people. But it contained, in clear and brief form, an expression of Jefferson's plan for government and left a permanent impression. The section prohibiting slavery in the new territory was voted down; but Jefferson's definite desire to exclude it from the Northwest Territory helped limit slavery's hold. It never flourished in that part of the country. Another bill he wrote was on the vexing question of coinage. Jefferson wanted to use Spanish dollars as a unit and have other coins valued by the decimal system—by tens. Robert Morris had a more elaborate plan in mind.

"Arithmetic troubles most people," Jefferson said, as the two talked about their plans. "When we can choose, we should always take the easy way." Smiling, Morris agreed.

Congress accepted Jefferson's plan, and that was the end of pounds and shillings and farthings in America. But alas! they did not accept his plans for equally simple systems of weights and measures.

On the seventh of May, 1784, while all these interesting matters were under way, Congress appointed Jefferson to be minister plenipotentiary to France and to help Franklin and Adams make trade agreements. He was ordered to Paris immediately.

Suddenly a door seemed to open onto a new life. Patsy would go with him. They would have a wonderful time.

chapter twelve

Ambassador to France

IN A FEW HOURS, Jefferson settled his household accounts and left Annapolis for Philadelphia.

"It is a pity," he remarked to James Monroe, "to leave all this important legislation—but my orders were imperative. The papers are ready, and this time there is no ice to delay the ship. I shall take Patsy with me."

The little girl was astonished at the news.

"*We* go to *Europe,* Papa!" she cried, her eyes wide. "Now?"

"We shall start for Boston as soon as possible—early to-morrow, I hope. Pack warm clothing for the voyage, Daughter, and your books and writing things . . ."

"But Polly?" Patsy asked. "And Baby Lucy, Papa?"

"They will continue to stay with your Aunt Eppes. I have written to her about my new plans. Aunt Carr will attend to plantation business—I shall close the house."

"Close Monticello, Papa? It will be lonely for us."

"We shall come back to it, never fear," Jefferson said, smiling. "It will be doubly dear after this long journey."

The drive to Boston in the phaeton took eighteen days, and all the way Jefferson observed fields and hamlets, towns and shops; he had not seen this part of the country. The travelers had many conversations, strange at Patsy's age.

"It is an odd thing," her father remarked one day, "that a farmer is chosen to do commercial business abroad."

"You buy and sell for our plantation, Papa," Patsy said.

"Yes, though that business is trifling compared to a nation's needs. But General Washington thinks I should go. Well, I shall do my best. Now we must practice our French, Patsy."

The day after they arrived in Boston, they sailed away in the *Ceres*. Patsy wrote to her aunt about the voyage:

> "We had a lovely passage on a beautiful new ship that had made but one passage before. There were only six passengers all of whom Papa knew and fine sunshine all the way with sea calm as a river. In the channel it rained violently all the way and the sea was exceedingly rough."

From Le Havre they drove to Paris in the phaeton, which had been shipped on the *Ceres*. At first sight France seemed like Virginia—good farms, fine harvests, people well fed. But when they changed horses in a village, beggars crowded so close that Patsy was frightened. The travelers were a mile or more on their way before either of them spoke.

"You have never seen such beggars in Virginia," Jefferson said, at last. Patsy sighed, relieved to hear his voice.

"But why here, Papa? This country is as fertile as Virginia." A farmer's daughter knew good land.

"Yes, but the government is different, Patsy. In America a man always has the hope that he can do better. In France there is a kind of caste system—once a merchant or farmer or beggar, a man always continues the same. And we do not have beggars, like these. In America they could work and make a living."

"I'm glad for America, Papa." Patsy smiled up at him.

On the third day they came to Paris, a city as beautiful as they had hoped it would be. The wide boulevards, the handsome bridges, buildings, parks, and quays, were like a dream. Only later did they discover slums and the hungry unemployed.

Jefferson called on Dr. Franklin, who helped him find a house. The new home was elegant, but it would be expensive to run. Jefferson wrote to James Monroe about his living:

> "I live here about as well as we did at Annapolis, but it takes my whole allowance. I ask nothing from the government for my time, but I think my expenses should be paid."

He had to borrow money to furnish the house, and he wrote home for cash from farm earnings to repay the loan.

One of Jefferson's greatest pleasures was the renewal of friendship with the Marquis de Lafayette. The two had worked together in war-torn Virginia in 1781. Now they could share many interests in a happier time.

Lafayette recommended a good convent school for Patsy, and soon she was entered there.

"I shall come and see you next Saturday," Jefferson promised her. Patsy clung to his hand—the place seemed so strange! She could not speak, and she would not cry as he left.

That autumn was delightful. Jefferson enjoyed the men Franklin and Lafayette knew; he shared parties, music, plays, and good talk. At home he had sought the friendship of Germans and Italians—his love of people was world-wide. But here he was with the French in their own land; that was even better.

But in the winter, the cold was hard on a Virginian. Word came that baby Lucy had died. How he wished that he had brought Polly with him. Day after day he was quite miserable.

By spring Jefferson had got into regular working habits, and his spirits improved. His mornings were for letters and interviews directly connected with his government work; afternoons for long walks in the city and countryside; evenings with people. He found interesting inventions: a lamp with a circular, oil-burning wick; and matches with phosphorus tips that would light without flint. He talked about these with Dr. Franklin.

"Man can do anything, make anything," Franklin said. "He has only to use the wits God gave him. I think some day men will fly." He chuckled with amusement. "But you should see people stare when I predict that. Well, time will tell!"

Sometimes Jefferson took Patsy to walk by the bookstalls

along the Left Bank. While he leafed through books and made purchases, she watched the boats on the Seine and the children rolling hoops in the park.

"How are you doing with Latin?" he asked her one day.

"Not so well, Papa," she admitted. "I *cannot* read Livy."

"Patsy! We can always do what we resolve to do."

"Yes, Papa," she said meekly. She knew he believed that and practiced it for himself.

"Remember, Daughter, it is a part of the American character to surmount every difficulty with resolution."

"I shall try harder, Papa. I am proud I am an American."

He held her hand tightly as they walked back to the convent; after all, she was only twelve and in a strange land. Polly should join them; they should be together. He wrote to Polly that same evening; he told her he loved her and missed her. He asked her to come to France. He mentioned a doll he had awaiting her. Little Polly had her mother's beauty but her father's temperament—kind but firm. She replied:

> "Dear Papa, I long to see you and hope that you and sister Patsy are well...you must come very soon and see us. I hope you will send me a doll. I am sorry you sent for me. I don't want to go to school in France, I had rather stay with Aunt Eppes.
> Your most happy and dutiful daughter,
> Polly Jefferson."

She kept to this decision through many letters, until finally her father decided that she should stay in Virginia.

Life was proving pleasant in Paris. A limited edition of

Jefferson's *Notes on the State of Virginia* was published—his
first and only book. The work was well received in France and
in England. When Dr. Franklin decided to retire, John Adams
was appointed the Minister to London and Jefferson was made
the Minister to France. Frenchmen were pleased.

"So you are replacing Dr. Franklin," the foreign secretary
said cordially, at the next official reception.

"No one can replace Dr. Franklin," Jefferson answered
quickly. "I merely succeed him." Frenchmen liked that tactful reply.

Indeed, America was fortunate to have men of education
and grace for her early ministers. Relations between the countries were difficult enough, even so. Many Frenchmen heartily
disliked Americans because war debts were unpaid and some
American traders made huge profits by sharp practices.

Jefferson's duties were strange, he thought; but he worked
at them diligently. He must see that whale oil, fish, and meats
were shipped to America on good terms. He must arrange for
selling rice, tobacco, and other American goods in France.

Jefferson never quite succeeded in making the trade treaties
that he tried to negotiate. But France did abolish some restrictions, and she was more co-operative than England was willing
to be. The two friends, Lafayette and Jefferson, worked tirelessly
for the welfare of their countries.

Hours of each day were needed for the hundreds of letters
that Jefferson wrote by hand. In one to James Monroe he urged
him to visit France:

"It will make you adore your own country, its soil, its climate, its equality, liberty, laws, manners. How little my countrymen know their blessings. I had no idea myself."

On his daily walks Jefferson talked with people of every way of life. He saw clearly that dire poverty was caused by twin evils—an extravagant government and that caste system which prevented men from bettering themselves. In 1785, France had huge estates and few small farm owners. He was glad Virginia was changing her laws; he believed more than ever that people who own their own homes and farms are the strength of a nation.

In the spring of 1786, Mr. Adams invited Jefferson to come to England to help make treaties with Tripoli. Jefferson did not expect a welcome; but he was astonished when the king actually turned his back on the author of the Declaration of Independence!

"I had expected that a king would have good manners," he remarked to Adams. As soon as he could leave London, he went to see the Shakespeare country.

On his travels he saw a mill run by steam, and he met Matthew Boulton, partner of the inventor, James Watts. A visit with these men repaid him for the discourtesy of the king.

In the spring of 1787, Jefferson decided to travel in southern France and Italy and he went to bid Patsy good-by.

"Perhaps I shall find new plants or ways of building houses that we can use at home," he told her as they walked. "Part of my work is to bring new ideas back to America."

"And you will talk with many people, Papa," Patsy said.

"You will discuss politics and find out how much they pay for rent and taxes. You will like that."

Her father looked down at her, surprised. Patsy was very knowing. Well, she was going on fifteen.

Jefferson was away for three months, and his notebooks bulged with facts. He talked with innkeepers and stableboys; with peasant farmers, as well as gentry.

Standing by a field one day, he watched a peasant drag a clumsy wooden plow through the earth. Its poor work annoyed him.

"What should a plow do?" he asked himself. "It must cut the soil, raise it up, and turn it over." Taking pencil and paper from his pocket, he quickly made a sketch, figured the problem by geometry, and then sketched again. The result was a pattern of a new type of moldboard, the curved front part of a plow. With a wave to the farmer, he went on.

Later he sent the drawing home, where a plow by that pattern was made, tested, and proved good. This was thought to be the first plow of such a shape. It was then made of wood, but later of metal, and was adopted generally.

At Nîmes the relics of Roman grandeur delighted Jefferson. He drew careful sketches that later were the inspiration for his designs for the capitol of Virginia at Richmond. His ardent love of classical art helped to bring about its revival in the United States.

During this time of travel, two unrelated events were taking place in America. The first was personal: Polly decided to go to France. With only the maid, Sally, the little girl set out on the long voyage to England, where Mrs. John Adams met her. Then, since he had to stay in Paris on business, Jefferson sent his trusted steward, Petit, to fetch her on the last lap of the journey.

The two daughters and their father had a happy reunion; then both girls went to the convent for studies. There Polly was welcomed by the friends Patsy had made.

"We cannot call you Mary or Pollee!" the little French girls said. "We shall call you Marie." So Polly had a third name and later a fourth, Maria. She chose this one herself and pronounced it "Ma-ree-a." It was her favorite.

The other event was the making of a constitution for the United States of America. Jefferson well knew how very much his country needed a good constitution; he had experienced many troubles under the inadequate Articles of Confederation. He knew most of the fifty-five men who were meeting in Philadelphia to write the constitution for the new republic. He wrote daily letters making suggestions, begging for news.

Even while this convention was meeting in America, Louis XVI, king of France, called his legislature to the palace. He wanted them to advise him about the sad state of France.

This later part of the eighteenth century was a time when people were beginning to think vigorously about government. Thoughtful men remarked that it was a pity Thomas Jefferson, with his knowledge and his genius for political science, could not share directly in the work for better government. The Atlantic separated him from the United States. Diplomatic courtesy kept him silent in France.

Lafayette came often to see Jefferson and to ask his advice, privately, in Jefferson's home. One day, the American saw it was necessary to be frank.

"I warn you, my friend," Jefferson said sternly. "Do not imitate the United States."

"Never did I expect to hear such words from you!" Lafayette shouted, astonished. "Our young men served in your armies; died in your battles. Inspiration for bettering our government came from America. And now you tell me not to follow your example!" His eyes fairly glittered as his quick temper flared.

"You would bring tragedy to France!" Jefferson's tone was polite, but firm. "You cannot make government free by an announcement, my friend. Freedom has to be earned. Your people are not ready; for centuries they have lived under a king—they do not know the responsibilities freedom lays upon a people.

"In America we had to learn to rule ourselves as we forged our independent way into a wilderness. We made settlements; our people served on church vestries, in town meetings, in local government. These have proved to be training schools for voters as well as for leaders. Do not break from your traditions too quickly, I beg of you, my friend!"

"We cannot endure the evils around us!" Lafayette cried.

"You will go farther if you move slowly," Jefferson warned. "Your king asks for counsel—meet with him."

"Faff! You ask too much!" Lafayette stalked out.

The next day he came back, begging pardon and asking for advice. Jefferson again urged him to meet the king halfway. Sometimes French leaders seemed to listen; often they did not.

Meanwhile Jefferson continued his letters to the constitution-makers, especially to Wythe, Madison, and Monroe. His thoughts were ever with them in their vital work for America.

It was December when a copy of the document reached Paris. Jefferson immediately shut himself up to study it.

"There is no bill of human rights!" he exclaimed aloud, when he had read it through. "They have left out the essential of good government!" He walked about, much disturbed.

But when he settled down to read again, Jefferson found the paper had many good points; the threefold branches of government, executive, legislative, judicial; the senate with equal votes for all states; the president's veto; the taxing power in the house, the group closest to the people. But the dangers of omission were plain: no bill of rights; no limit to the length of office for a president—these seemed to Jefferson to be the worst.

"Men and parties should rotate," he told himself. "Power corrupts. But a perfect constitution cannot be expected immediately. It can be improved as time shows its faults to our nation."

Through more than a year Jefferson steadily wrote long letters to America, backing up the work of Madison, Washington, and others who labored for ratification of the Constitution. He tried to soothe Patrick Henry, who kept Virginia from ratifying. Henry attacked many of the very faults Jefferson saw, and he lacked faith in future improvements.

Jefferson found it hard to have much influence at long range. When he had worked on Virginia's new laws, he had been there and could meet arguments directly.

In March of 1788, a new task was given him, and Jefferson laid aside his desk work to journey to Holland. Here, with John Adams, he was to arrange for a great loan for the United

States. The plan was to borrow money on a business basis. With that cash in its treasury, the United States could pay debts and make better foreign trade agreements. As soon as taxes collected under the new Constitution began coming in, the loan would be paid back.

Jefferson and Adams managed this business skillfully and did an important service for their country. Now French soldiers and officers could collect their war wages—long overdue—for their fighting in America. That pleased Jefferson.

Soon after Jefferson came back from Holland, he had three visitors, young college men of Virginia. They had been studying in Edinburgh, and they stopped in Paris briefly on their way home. One was Thomas Mann Randolph, son of Jefferson's cousin who had lived at Tuckahoe. Patsy and Maria came from school to be hostesses. Thomas Mann and Patsy were attracted to each other, and after the visitors went home the two corresponded. But romance by sailing ship was dull; Patsy pined for Virginia.

By the spring of 1789, Jefferson decided that they must go home. Maria, too, was homesick. For himself, he longed to talk with American friends. Paris was torn with political strife, and it was impossible to continue a neutral.

George Washington was inaugurated as President in April, and soon after that, Jefferson wrote for permission to visit home. The President assented at once; but slow mail, the task of packing the many things bought for Monticello, and other disappointments delayed the voyage until autumn.

Eleven-year-old Maria was not a good sailor. So again it was devoted Patsy who tramped the deck with her impatient father and listened to his talk.

"Our country will be changed," he said one day. "Our republic now has a constitution and a president. I hope it is going like this good ship—full sail and straight ahead toward a free government for all the people."

"Yes, Papa," Patsy said, her eyes turned to the west. Suddenly she clutched his sleeve.

"Look, Papa! That long gray line! It's *land!* I'll call Maria—Papa, we've come home!"

chapter thirteen

Mr. Secretary

CROWDS SURGED around the returning travelers as they landed.
Stevedores began taking off luggage; bystanders who recognized
the tall man with two daughters came to welcome them and
lingered to hear news of France. As soon as he could, Jefferson
got a newspaper and avidly scanned the pages. Patsy noticed
that something disturbed him.

"Is something wrong at home, Papa?" she asked.

"No. No, Patsy—for I shall not accept." He folded the

paper and put it in his pocket. "I read that President Washington wants me to be Secretary of State."

"Oh, Papa! Then you would be nearer home!" Patsy exclaimed.

"But my work in France is unfinished. Say no more. I shall not accept." He turned to the unloading of boxes.

The journey across Virginia was slow, for friends and relatives along the way wanted to entertain the travelers. The Jeffersons were visiting Aunt Eppes when an express messenger from President Washington caught up with them and delivered a formal invitation to serve in the new cabinet. "The work involves many of the most interesting objects of executive authority," the President explained as an inducement.

This request could not be hastily put aside. Jefferson answered that he liked his work in France but would do what Washington thought best. "You are to marshall us for the public good," he wrote. Then they continued on their way to Monticello.

A rider was sent ahead with orders to have the house warm and ready. Two days later, the Jeffersons came to Shadwell. There runners set out for Monticello with the glad news. By the time the carriage reached the foot of the mountain it was surrounded by shouting crowds.

"Marster Jefferson's come home!"

"He's here!"

"Welcome home!"

Young men unhitched the horses and pulled the carriage

up the mountain road. Women and children ran alongside, singing and shouting gleefully. At the east door, Jefferson was half pulled from the phaeton and carried into the house on the shoulders of his "people." Others carried Patsy and Polly. It was a joyous homecoming for all.

But when Jefferson inspected his plantations, later, joy turned to anxiety. Everything was run down. He had been away too long. The Paris debts could not be paid by these depleted farms. He saw that he should stay at home and earn a living.

Then Madison came over and was persuasive. And Washington wrote that Jefferson was needed in the cabinet.

"The President suffered losses in war service, too," Jefferson said to his family. "I can do no less for a new republic." So he accepted the office of secretary of state and promised Washington that he would come to New York as soon as his daughter was married.

On the twenty-third of February, 1790, the Randolph and Jefferson families gathered at Monticello for the marriage of Martha (Patsy) Jefferson and her second cousin, Thomas Mann Randolph. The young couple, both tall and good-looking, were radiantly happy. The bride's father was pleased that she had chosen a husband of fine mind and education. And, too, the young people were to live at Monticello, for Thomas Mann had agreed to manage Jefferson's farms while his father-in-law served in the cabinet.

A week later, Jefferson left home for his new duties. He

stopped at Philadelphia to give Dr. Franklin news of Paris; then he hastened on to New York, where he rented a modest house. He had had to borrow two thousand dollars for expenses, and his small salary gave little hope of saving for repayment.

New Yorkers welcomed the distinguished man, newly come from France. Washington greeted him warmly. Dinners were given in his honor. But the talk at parties astonished Jefferson.

"We should stop this silly notion of republican government before it is too late," some said. "America needs a king."

"A *king?*" Jefferson was shocked. "A king in America?" He certainly had been away from his country too long!

"Mr. Jefferson has just arrived," the host remarked quickly. "He will soon see that a mob is not to be trusted."

"Do people really feel this distrust?" Jefferson asked.

"Oh, yes, there are more monarchists than republicans!"

"The idea of the mob *electing* a ruler is ridiculous!"

As he heard such ideas repeated day after day, Jefferson began to see that many New Yorkers truly believed that a monarchy was the best form of government. They distrusted the common citizen. New York, he thought, had been influenced by long British occupation during the war. Did the whole nation, Virginia, Pennsylvania, New England, long for a monarchy like England's? Jefferson felt sure that it did not.

As for the new government, Jefferson saw that a great deal had been done since Washington had become President. A bill of rights was added to the Constitution. A start was made toward better finances. The cabinet was set up. Jefferson studied this group carefully at his first meeting with them.

The President sat erect in the chairman's place. He looked older than his fifty-eight years; war service had impaired his health. General Knox, plump and forty, was Secretary of War. Edmund Randolph, forty-three and a Virginian, was Attorney General. The Secretary of the Treasury, Alexander Hamilton, the youngest and most vigorous cabinet member, was thirty-three; a West Indian who had come to New York at fifteen to educate himself and seek his fortune. He had served as aide to Washington during the war, and the President trusted his keen mind. Jefferson, the new member, was forty-seven; he was tall, lean, and experienced. His manner was easy and informal.

This meeting was to study national finances. Hamilton, at the request of Congress, had made a plan. He had presented the first part of it in January; Jefferson had known of that before he left Virginia. Hamilton had listed the national debts:

 $11,710,378 due to foreigners for war debts
  42,414,085 due Americans for war debts
   2,000,000 other debts
 $56,124,463 total debt.

Hamilton proposed to sell government bonds and pay these debts in full. The cabinet members seemed to accept his plan, and Hamilton remarked that a debt was a good thing for a nation, as it helped keep a country together.

Jefferson listened and wondered. On his way north he had

heard many arguments about who was to get the money the government paid for a debt.

"Take my Aunt Mattie," a man at a tavern had said. "Her husband was killed in the war. She got certificates for his war pay; but she needed cash, not paper. A man came along and bought them for a quarter of the printed value—paid fifty dollars for two hundred. If the government pays back that two hundred, who gets it? Aunt Mattie or that man?"

"The man who bought it of her," a Hamilton supporter said promptly. "She was glad to sell, wasn't she?"

Men in the tavern had protested.

"I know a merchant who sold his crop to the government," another said. "He was paid with certificates. He couldn't run his farm with paper money; so he sold—ten cents on a dollar was the best he could get. The government knows his name— who will get this new pay, now?"

"The man who has the certificates," the Hamilton man said.

Many citizens were not satisfied; but the bill had passed. Bonds were bought, and debts were paid off. National credit improved; trade picked up. Hamilton's promises seemed justified.

The next step, talked of at this very cabinet meeting, was paying state war debts. No one knew exactly how much these were; Hamilton guessed twenty million dollars. He proposed that the government assume these debts; he called his plan the Assumption Bill. It had made bitter talk because some states owed more, and so would profit more, than others. The bill had recently been defeated in Congress—by two votes.

A few days later Jefferson went to keep an appointment with the President and chanced to meet Hamilton on the way.

"Good morning, Mr. Jefferson!" Hamilton's handsome face was alight and friendly. "May I have a word with you?"

"Certainly!" But Jefferson wondered at the request.

"What are we to do about these seceding states, sir?"

"Seceding states!" Jefferson was astonished. "Surely—"

"You have not been here long enough to understand," Hamilton interrupted. He took Jefferson's arm and led him down the street as he talked. "The Assumption Bill is making hard feelings; especially in those states that have paid off part of their debts. We *have* to have that bill to keep the country united. For the sake of national credit all state debts must be paid now." They walked to the corner, and Hamilton turned back. He held Jefferson's arm as he talked of his theories and hopes.

"Really, sir"—Jefferson tried to stop at Washington's doorstep—"I have not had time to learn the amount."

"Twenty million will cover it"—Hamilton waved his free hand—"a small price to pay for unity. If we sweeten it up, the South will change her votes . . . "

"Sweeten it?" Jefferson interrupted. He wondered if he caught the word right. "This is not the time and place to talk; the President expects me. Come to my house—say, dinner tomorrow?"

"Agreed. May I bring a friend or two?" Jefferson nodded, smiling. Perhaps, talking quietly, they could work out some plan.

After dinner the next day, the cloth was removed and political talk began. Jefferson listened carefully.

"A new location is proposed for the nation's capital," Hamilton began. "Many places are trying to get the honor. I now propose to present two bills to Congress at the same time: one, the Assumption Bill; the other, a bill to locate the capital on the Potomac River. I'll suggest that it be in Philadelphia for ten years until a suitable city can be built. You two gentlemen are from the Potomac section—what do you say to my suggestion?"

He turned to the two congressmen who had voted against his bill. They were silent, thoughtful. Hamilton had power; they could not hold out against him. Southerners might as well get something—if only a new city. With shamed faces they agreed to change their votes. The Assumption Bill would pass—and the new capital would be in the South.

Jefferson was chagrined that this "deal" was made in his house. The controversy, and many others, too, made him unhappy. He missed his home and his daughters; they seldom wrote. In a letter to Martha he said:

"I am anxious to hear from you. Do not neglect your music. It will be a companion many hours of life. Having had yourself and dear Poll to live with me, I feel the separation from you."

But he was glad they were at Monticello.

The next week he wrote to Maria:

"Where are you, my dear Maria? How do you do? How are you occupied? Write me by the first post and tell me—do you see the sun rise every day? How many pages do you read? Do you know how to make a pudding, cut a beefsteak, sow spinach or set a hen? Be good, my dear, as I have always found you . . . then all the world will love you, and I more than all the world . . . Adieu my dear Maria.

Th. Jefferson."

Eleven-year-old Maria replied in her serious style:

"Dear Papa, I have not been able to read Don Quixote every-day as I have been traveling [visiting relatives] since you went away and the dictionary is too large for the pocket of the chariot . . . I am reading Robertson's America. I thank you for the advice . . . I will try to follow it. Adieu, dear Papa.

Maria Jefferson."

As he read the letter he imagined her pretty face, bent over the paper, as she tried to form each letter correctly.

Soon he was settled in bachelor quarters. He tried to live simply, but his position required much entertaining. His salary of $3,500 was not nearly enough, and Monticello farms would not make a profit for some time.

The work of the new Secretary of State was to organize a foreign service and oversee domestic business that was not directly connected with war or navy or finance. Along with these duties, Jefferson began to work with the President in planning for a Federal City on the Potomac. The two Virginians conferred often; Jefferson made sketches; they engaged L'Enfant, the French architect; and together they visited the site where someday a beautiful city was to rise from a swamp.

Other duties were less congenial, for, as time went by, Jefferson felt a growing uneasiness about his country.

Hamilton's plans were bringing material prosperity. National credit was good. Settlers in the West made their corn into whisky, because in that form it was easy to market. The tax on that whisky put money in the national treasury, but Jefferson wondered whether such a tax was a wise way to get money for his country.

Factories, shops, and mills prospered. But workers in such places did not seem concerned about liberty and equality. In Virginia, farmers had talked of such subjects daily.

Near the end of 1790 the banking bill passed, and a National Bank of the United States, modeled on the Bank of England, was set up. Bonds were sold; businessmen got loans; the new republic prospered. But most Americans still kept their savings in a cookie jar.

Jefferson had opposed that bank. He thought it put too much power into the hands of a few men. He feared it would build up a moneyed class. At this time, less than a year after Jefferson returned from France, the differences in political thinking between Hamilton and Jefferson came into the open.

Both were brilliant men and honest patriots. But Hamilton believed government should be controlled by a few; he distrusted the ignorance of the common people. Jefferson distrusted the selfishness of rulers; he had faith in the common people. His remedy for their ignorance was education. From this time on, the two men became intense rivals.

Rumors of this rivalry got around, and men took sides. Those who wanted a strong central government in control of national finances called themselves Federalists. Others, like Jefferson, who had faith in people and wanted a truly republican government called themselves Republicans.

Feeling grew so violent that Jefferson tried to resign and so remove strife from the cabinet. But Washington would not let him go; he felt the country needed both men.

Then the time drew near for Washington's term to end. He was eager to be free. The nation was torn with conflict. England and France were quarreling. The neutrality that the President ordered was difficult, because Hamilton ardently admired England and the sympathies of Jefferson and many Revolutionary War veterans were with France.

"Washington is the only man who can hold this country together!" men said.

"Somebody must make Washington run again! We can trust him. Ask Tom Jefferson to persuade him," others said.

In September of that campaign year, 1792, Jefferson stopped at Mount Vernon overnight. Before breakfast the next morning, the two friends sat on the wide new veranda and had a quiet talk.

"If I take the office again, I shall want you to be my Secretary of State," Washington said.

"Oh, you can easily fill my place," Jefferson told him.

"No, I want *you,*" the President insisted. "Though I can understand your desire to resign. I have no liking for office myself."

Jefferson nodded agreement and added: "Why should you want to leave this beautiful home?"

"But the call of duty is strong. You feel it, my friend. I shall mediate between you and Mr. Hamilton. I need you both."

A call for breakfast ended the talk. Jefferson had half agreed to continue in office.

Months passed. Bitterness between rival factions grew. Jefferson began to feel that he could do more for his country at home, writing, than he could by serving on that cabinet. On the last day of December, 1793, he wrote to the President:

"I now take the liberty of resigning the office into your hands. I carry into my retirement a lively sense of your goodness."

The President accepted, with equal graciousness. The two men remained firm friends.

Jefferson was deeply depressed as he left for home.

"Never again shall I accept a public office," he decided. "I am not fitted. I have failed twice." But as he drove mile after mile, he wondered what anyone else could have done. Britain had broken her promise to vacate western lands. France needed help a weak young nation could not give. Americans seemed more interested in making money than in their country.

Where were the once vivid dreams of equality for all men? Where was the moral force that had kept men fighting in the Revolutionary War? Were these gone forever?

chapter fourteen

A Bitter Campaign

AFTER DAYS of lonely driving, Jefferson rounded the mountain, and Monticello loomed ahead. Maria, looking like her mother, ran out to greet him. Martha stood on the east steps, little Ann, now three, clinging to her skirts, and Thomas Jefferson Randolph in her arms. Suddenly cares of state dropped away. Jefferson ran up those steps like a boy.

Soon Farmer Jefferson took up his work with eagerness. Growing things brought healing, and his plantations needed him.

Of the more than ten thousand acres he owned, only about two thousand were being farmed; that was a usual division between wild and used land, then. The fields in use, sadly worn by one-crop tobacco-planting, had to support many people; the Jefferson and Carr families, nearly two hundred slaves, and countless visitors. Of the slaves about three-quarters were workers; the others were the old or the young.

These workers provided almost everything needed on the place. Men were carpenters, blacksmiths, brickmakers, masons, cabinetworkers, and farmers. They made the bricks, nails, and woodwork of the fine house. Women carded wool, spun, wove, and made garments; they gardened, baked, canned, and preserved.

While in France, Jefferson had learned much about farming methods. Between affairs of state, Jefferson and Washington had often talked about such matters. Both planters were interested in crop rotation to build up the soil, contour planting to stop erosion, and new machinery and tools.

Jefferson divided his plantation into four farms, each subdivided into smaller farms of about forty acres. These were to be planted in wheat, corn, rye, buckwheat, and clover, in rotation. Each of the four large farms had its overseer and workers.

While all this was getting under way, days were pleasantly distracted by visitors. Martha and her family lived at Edgehill, nearby, and came over often; young Carrs were married and made long visits on the mountain. Sister Anna had married while her brother was in France; now she spent summers at Monticello.

James Madison was a favorite among the many friends who came, though he often left his host a bit unsettled.

"You should let us work and elect you President," Madison said casually, one day, as though half joking. "I should like to see you take hold of the mess." Jefferson laughed that off, but the idea lingered. Madison meant that it should.

Men who wrote letters were more direct. "You must come back into politics, Mr. Jefferson," they said. "We need you."

"I take care of letters easily," he remarked to Maria. "I act like a farmer and wait for a rainy day to reply."

But some letters pricked him. The Federalists believed that the people needed to be governed "for their own good." Jefferson trusted the common people. He wrote, "Mankind should have as much liberty as each may exercise without injuring the liberty of his fellow citizens."

Because individual liberty was important to him, Jefferson was shocked when Britain impressed American seamen for service on British ships. He watched eagerly for news, after the President sent John Jay to England to protest. But the weak treaty Jay brought home early in 1795 gave no protection to American seamen or ships.

"Hamilton, with his devotion to England, is partly responsible for this!" Jefferson said when he read his newspaper. "How long will Americans endure such treatment?" There was angry public clamor; but the treaty was ratified. Hamilton had resigned his office and gone to New York to build up his fortune—he was a brilliant lawyer. Washington had trouble filling the cabinet; public office gave men neither money nor prestige, it seemed.

But from New York, Hamilton continued to have influence in strengthening the federal government. In spite of efforts to detach himself, Jefferson read papers, answered letters, and had a concern for the people. He wrote to Congressman Madison begging him to "stop Hamilton!"

In 1796, when Washington's Farewell Address settled the question of a third term, people began to talk about a successor. At taverns, after church, at dinners, this was the main topic.

"John Adams will run for the Federalists," a city man would say. "And he will listen to Jay and Hamilton."

"Adams is safe for us businessmen."

But outside of cities men had other thoughts.

"We should have a Republican," farmers said. "We should put up Tom Jefferson. He's for the people."

"I heard he's retired."

"Well, let's bring him back. He's our best man."

Federalists chose Adams and Pinckney for their candidates, and Republicans put up Jefferson and Aaron Burr. Madison could not promise that their candidate would accept—but no objections came from Monticello. And no help, either. Thomas Jefferson waited.

At that time each party put up two men, on the theory that both must be capable of serving as President. Of the four, the one who got the high vote was elected President; the second highest, Vice-President. They might be of opposing parties—and so it happened this time.

When the votes were counted in February, Adams had seventy-one and Jefferson sixty-eight.

"Two votes the other way and our man would have won!" Republicans exclaimed, astonished at the near-victory.

"But will Jefferson take second place?" men worried. "He's a good man. He should have won."

The country soon found that Thomas Jefferson was reasonable and not too proud. He would be Vice-President. He saw that the new Congress was Federalist; as President, he could have accomplished little toward advancing his own ideas.

Jefferson planned to slip into Philadelphia unobserved. But word of his coming got around, and he was met by a crowd of admirers and a parade. Men carried banners which said:

JEFFERSON, FRIEND OF THE PEOPLE

They escorted him all the way to his lodgings.

On March fourth, 1797, the new Vice-President took the oath of office in the Senate room and made a few gracious remarks. Men saw that Jefferson was vigorous and well; farming had been good for him. His red hair had grayed a bit, but he was erect and walked with assurance.

In the House room, General Washington stood aside, tactfully seeking the background, while John Adams was sworn in and made his address. Adams was plainly pleased with his speech and its reception. That night he wrote to his wife

Abigail that "the address was the sublimest thing ever heard in America."

The Vice-President's task of presiding over the Senate was a dull job. So Jefferson interested himself in compiling rules of parliamentary procedure; his text was used for many years. He was elected president of the American Philosophical Society —an office he held for a long time. His nephew, John Eppes,

one of the cousins Maria had played with as a child, came to live and study with his uncle. In the summer Jefferson took a house out by the Schuylkill River; Maria came to stay with him, and the three had meals and happy hours under the trees.

As months went by, Jefferson began to see that if he was to be a successful champion of the liberties of the common people, he must have a political party behind him. Men in this party must be informed, enthusiastic, and well organized. So he began to build such an organization. Men who believed as he did wrote newspaper articles, organized clubs, and got friends interested.

These Anti-Federalists now called their party "Republican" because that was the form of government set up by the Constitution; that is, voters elected officials to represent them and govern the nation. This party stood for the rights of common, everyday people to rule. It was against large public debt, and against a strong central federal power that might come to be ruled by a few men.

Of course Federalists lived in a republic, too. Differences between the parties came about through the interpretation of the Constitution and the emphasis upon what, to each, was important.

The Federalists believed in strong federal power controlled by "the wise and the good," as it was expressed. That is, by men of birth and education who should be given power to govern the nation. Federalists had their party organization, too, their newspapers and their devoted workers.

Their party was also in office. When political debates grew bitter they passed the Alien and Sedition Act to give President Adams almost unlimited power over free speech. It became a crime to criticize the President, but the Vice-President was not so protected. Shocking tales were printed about him.

One day a friend brought a certain newspaper to Jefferson.

"This paper calls you a scoundrel, an atheist!" he cried. "You must assert yourself!"

"I would need twenty clerks and all my time for that!" Jefferson answered. "I can wait for the good sense of my countrymen to prevail." Many thought him far too patient.

Madison worked out a bill guarding free speech in Virginia. A similar bill passed in Kentucky. Free speech became an important issue in the next campaign.

Meanwhile foreign affairs were a serious problem for President Adams. Jay's weak treaty pleased few of his countrymen. Then there was the question of neutrality between warring France and England and of the shocking preying upon American ships. France took three hundred ships to keep their cargoes from getting to England. Americans were furious.

Fortunately President Adams was able to work out disputes and make a treaty just in time to avert what seemed certain war.

Through all these troubled times, Jefferson managed to get away from Philadelphia occasionally to enjoy the quiet he craved at Monticello. While he was Vice-President Maria married John Eppes and went to live at Eppington, the place she had loved as a child. They came often to visit her father at Monticello. Martha now had several children who came there, too.

"I am fortunate in having two sons-in-law who are handsome, educated, and agreeable," Jefferson remarked to his sister Anna. "But I do need a larger house for my big family."

Many times since his return from France he had wanted to continue work on his house, but time and money were lacking. Jefferson had never thought of Monticello as finished; now he meant to get at the work. On one vacation he had a brick kiln set up again and got a nail factory going.

Jefferson's notebook was full of sketches of buildings which he had drawn in Europe. With these for inspiration, he drew new plans. He sketched a dome and deep bay windows. He designed beds set in walls. His own bed pulled up out of the way when not in use. This work was a rest from political turmoil.

While he was doing this architectural work, Jefferson was also building public opinion through countless letters. He stated in these exactly what he believed in for his country:

A government that is simple and thrifty
Free commerce among nations
Freedom of religion and the press
Support for the Constitution
Every power left to the state unless actually given to the federal government by the Constitution.

Jefferson assured all: "The first object of my heart is my own country."

Such clear, plain words endeared him to the people; even the uneducated could understand. They felt Thomas Jefferson's confidence in them—in farmers, frontiersmen, the thousands of untaught, unknown, who by their courage and hard work had built America. These people wanted Jefferson to be their President.

In the party caucus, Jefferson was nominated, with Aaron Burr for his running mate. Federalists nominated John Adams and Charles Pinckney. And the bitter campaign began.

There were loyal patriots in both parties, but they differed violently on how to attain their political ideals. Federalists were sure the nation must have a strong central power or it would fall apart. Republicans argued for free speech and more power in the states. With Jefferson, they believed that the closer to the people government stayed, the safer for all.

In the stress of this bitter campaign Jefferson wrote a battle cry that was to be long remembered:

"I have sworn on the altar of God eternal hostility against every form of tyranny over the mind of man."

When at last the votes were counted, Americans found that Adams was defeated—but Jefferson was not elected. He and Burr had seventy-three electoral votes each for President. That sort of tie, in the same party, had never been foreseen.

In city and hamlet, by roadside and wharf, people talked of this strange result. Some looked up the Constitution.

"The election must be decided in the House of Representatives," they reported.

"How will it come out?"

No one knew. Half dazed, the country waited.

chapter fifteen

The Third President

THE CAPITAL CITY of the United States of America had been moved from Philadelphia to its new site by the Potomac River in June of 1800. But as yet it had none of the dignity and beauty Washington and Jefferson hoped for when they engaged L'Enfant to draw up the plans. Crowds attracted to the city by the novelty of a presidential election in the House of Representatives were dismayed at what they saw that February of 1801.

Trees had been cut, and streets laid out. But the hundreds of stumps were unsightly; streets were mere rutted lanes winding between stumps and trash. The President's house looked attractive; and a mile east, on a hill, the foundations and one wing of the Capitol were up. Hastily built boardinghouses near Capitol Hill were crowded. Legislators and visitors who could not get lodgings had to live in Georgetown, three miles away—with stumps, chuckholes, and mud cluttering the crude road they must travel to and fro.

Vice-President Jefferson was living in Conrad's boardinghouse, and fellow boarders were frankly partisan.

"Of course if it was a tie between Adams and Jefferson, I'd feel different," a man down the table explained. "But the Republican caucus nominated Jefferson for President—Burr knows that as well as I do."

"Exactly! He's not dumb. Just got his head turned by landing so near the top." A chuckle went around the table.

"They're saying now that the Federalists will let Tom win if he'll promise—"

"Tom Jefferson won't promise anything to get elected. Not he! I've heard him say that, and he means it."

"Here he comes, now. What's the latest vote, Mr. Jefferson?"

"Eight to six, and two states not voting—no majority," Jefferson replied cheerfully, and pulled up a chair.

The voting had been going on for days—always the same. The nation was getting restless; the feeling grew more tense. Alexander Hamilton knew that the deadlock must end. He distrusted Burr personally; he feared the political aims of

Jefferson. But as the futile balloting continued, he threw his considerable influence to his one-time opponent, and Thomas Jefferson was elected President on the thirty-sixth ballot.

When the result was announced, on the seventeenth day of February, the town went wild, celebrating.

But while the Republicans rejoiced, Federalists were fearful for the future of the nation. They believed that Jefferson would ruin the United States.

Through that February, President Adams filled every office under his control with loyal Federalists. By March third he had appointed two hundred and sixteen new officials in what came to be known as the "Midnight appointments." The most shocking affront to Jefferson personally was the appointment of John Marshall as Chief Justice of the United States—a life office. Marshall was a Virginian, an ardent Federalist, and a bitter political foe of the new President. As Chief Justice he could defeat many of Jefferson's cherished aims.

The appointments made, Adams left town.

The morning of March fourth, 1801, the sun shone brightly on stumps, mud, and crowds of citizens who came by horse, coach, and wagon. In the boardinghouse, Jupiter felt a deep responsibility for the occasion. Gray stockings, green breeches and waistcoat were laid on the bed. A best coat hung on a chair as Jupiter barbered his hero.

Jefferson's thoughts were not on clothes, but on what this day might mean in history. It was the beginning of a new administration which was frankly for the common people.

"A revolution has taken place, Jupiter," he said. "A revolution without bloodshed."

"Yes, sir," Jupiter agreed. "Thanks to you, Marster Tom."

"No, not to me, Jupiter. To an ideal. To the ideal fought for in the War." Jupiter slipped on his coat. "Today's bitterness will pass. Free men will make a sound republican government that will safeguard our people and be an example to the world."

"Yes, Marster Tom. Now shall I call a coach?"

"No, I shall walk; it's only a short way." He set off briskly toward Capitol Hill.

Crowds streaming by recognized the man they had come to see—a tall, rangy figure, head held slightly forward.

"Looks like he's trying to see what's ahead," one man said.

"I hear he's the smartest man in America. Knows everything—farming, figuring, surveying, law, and a lot else. They say he reads even science books as though he liked 'em."

"Well, it's not spoiled him. He wouldn't sit at the head of the table this morning at Conrad's—and him the President, almost. I count on that man to run the country fair—like he said in the Declaration twenty-five years ago."

Jefferson entered the crowded Senate chamber amid loud applause. Republicans had a majority in both houses; many Federalists had gone home even before Adams left.

Walking forward, Jefferson shook hands with Burr, who had taken the oath as Vice-President a few minutes earlier. Chief Justice Marshall stood close by, Bible in hand. The room was hushed; all felt the drama as this man, appointed in deliberate defiance to Jefferson, was now to administer the sacred oath of office.

But both men were patriots and gentlemen. They gave no sign of enmity. Jefferson repeated the words that made him President. Then he stepped to the rostrum, glanced over the hushed audience, and began to speak. His voice, often husky, was clear, but low.

"Friends and Fellow Citizens:

Called upon to undertake the duties of the first executive office of our country, I express my grateful thanks. I humble myself before the magnitude of the undertaking and look to you for guidance."

Men leaned forward to catch his words. He was saying that he hoped the election bitterness would pass; honest differences of opinion did not mean differences of principles. His plea for unity sounded reassuring.

The President made clear his faith in government by the people. "I know," he explained, "that some honest men fear that a republican government cannot be strong; that this government is not strong enough. But would the honest patriot abandon a government that has so far kept us free and firm? I trust not. I believe this the strongest government on earth.

"Let us then, with courage and confidence pursue our own federal and republican principles, our union and representative government."

He then stated clearly his aims for the administration: Equal justice for all; friendship between nations; support of state government; rule by the majority; the supremacy of the civil over the military authority; economy . . . honest payment of our debts . . .

Men leaned back, relieved, as Jefferson went on to speak of ideals they had approved in the campaign—freedom of speech, of the press, of religion, and said "these principles form the bright constellation which has gone before us, and guided our steps through an age of revolution and reformation."

He closed in a reverent mood:

"And may that Infinite Power which rules the destinies of the universe, lead our councils to what is best, and give them a favorable issue for your peace and prosperity."

When he had finished, the President bowed to the applause and left the room. Friends walked back to Conrad's with him for dinner. But, by his request, there was no celebration.

Jefferson was in a fine mood.

"May I congratulate you, sir?" one of the boarders asked.

"Better wait a year," Jefferson grinned, as he helped himself to fried chicken. "You can tell better then."

As soon as possible the address was printed in newspapers. It was widely read. Republicans, of course, approved heartily. Federalists were pleased with its moderate tone. Perhaps the country would not be ruined as quickly under Jefferson as they had feared.

Two weeks later Jefferson moved into the White House. Someday this would be a handsome mansion; but now it was unfinished. The gleaming white sandstone looked odd set in grounds dotted with stumps and bordered with a rough fence.

The new President soon found that the roof leaked; the furniture was shabby after twelve years of hard use, and there was not enough for this larger house. Jefferson bought a few plain chairs to help out. The East Room was a mere shell, but he managed to make his office comfortable.

"I wish we had growing things here, Jupiter," Jefferson said one day. "Could you find some plants? I'd tend them."

"Yes, Marster Tom. I'll find us some." From that day a window-garden began, gradually shutting out the ugly view. A little later a burst of song greeted the President as he entered the room—a mockingbird? He must be dreaming! But there it was, singing in a cage above the window-garden.

"No, sir, I'll not tell how I got it." Jupiter chuckled when questioned. "You jes' listen to it sing, that's all." The bird became a pet, and when Jefferson was alone, he let it fly about the room as it sang.

Fate seemed kind to the new President. France had stopped fighting. Napoleon Bonaparte had made a treaty with England. At the moment there was peace, and Jefferson had a chance to organize his administration.

For his cabinet the President chose congenial, loyal men from various parts of the country. James Madison was appointed Secretary of State. This brilliant lawyer and lifelong friend was tactful and a good companion. His charming wife, Dolly Madison, could act as the President's hostess, if needed.

Albert Gallatin, a Swiss who had come to Pennsylvania in

his teens, was chosen Secretary of the Treasury. Gallatin was a financial genius and had been a Republican leader in the House. He believed that the nation's business should be presented simply so people could understand how their money was spent; he had organized the Ways and Means committee to help make this possible.

Another cabinet member was Attorney General Levi Lincoln, the famous veteran who had represented Washington at the surrender of Yorktown. Lincoln was from Massachusetts and Harvard. Postmaster Gideon Granger was from Connecticut and Yale; Secretary of War Henry Dearborn, of Maine, was a veteran; and Secretary of the Navy Robert Smith was a Baltimore shipper.

This important business was not yet completed when social problems had the town buzzing with rumors.

"I hear the President is having no levees," the wife of a Federalist exclaimed.

"He has to! Washington and Adams always had morning receptions each Tuesday," a friend retorted.

"The man must be a barbarian!" another cried.

"Ladies! We must take a stand! We shall call at the White House next Tuesday." They went in a body.

"The President is riding, ladies," the doorman told them. "Please come in. He will return soon."

The ladies were there, waiting, when the President got back. He was in riding clothes, of course, booted and dusty.

"This is an unexpected pleasure." He greeted them graciously. "I wish I had enough chairs for you. But do stay. It is so kind of you to call."

They lingered briefly—and that was the last levee.

Tales about Jefferson became a fad; people regaled each other with them. A favorite was about a man from Connecticut. This visitor chanced upon a man who wore an ordinary brown suit, but rode a fine horse.

"Wouldn't you like to trade that horse?" the visitor asked.

"Frankly, I would not," the brown-suiter said. "Why?"

"I want a good horse to get me out of town fast. I hate that man Jefferson!"

"Ever seen him?"

"No, but I'd know him anywhere. The hypocrite pretends to be for the people, but he wears costly clothes, two watches, and rings on every finger."

"You may have been misinformed, sir. The President dresses no better than I do. It happens that business takes me to the White House tomorrow. Meet me there at ten, and you may see the man."

"I went at ten," the Connecticut man often recounted. "My rider friend was near the door. But before he could speak to me, a servant approached with a letter.

"'Mr. President,' the servant began. I heard no more. I turned and ran—nearly killed myself on those rickety steps!"

There were many arguments about Jefferson's "simplicity." Many said that he was acting a part, and in a sense he was. Thomas Jefferson, the Virginia aristocrat, liked elegance and grace. He was one of the very few Americans who had lived in aristocratic circles in France. But as President of a republic he refused to set himself above any other citizen. He wore a brown coat, gray waistcoat, green velveteen breeches, and yarn stockings. His shoes were ordinary, and he often wore heelless slippers. He looked like a farmer of that time.

By autumn people were getting used to their President. Martha brought her children for a visit. Girls and boys raced in the White House halls, and the grim mansion began to seem like a home.

Then the time arrived for Congress to meet, and governing began in earnest.

chapter sixteen

President Jefferson at Work

NOW THAT THE GOVERNMENT was organized, President Jefferson was ready for work on his first big project—economy and the national debt. By electing him their leader, the voters had told him that they did not approve Hamilton's idea that debt was good for a nation. The United States was an agricultural country; and to farmers, debt meant interest, high taxes, and a mortgage on the future.

In one of his conferences with Secretary Gallatin the President restated his ideas.

"Debt has a way of growing," he said. "The time may come when our people will have to work too many days for their government. When they can keep less money for themselves, their standard of living will come down. If we are not careful, we shall be taxed in our meat, our drink, our necessaries and our comforts, in our labors and our amusements."

"I never agreed with Hamilton that people should not be told details of government finances," Gallatin said. "Government money is the people's money. They should know beforehand the plan for spending. Then they can object, if they wish."

So the President and Gallatin set down plain statements everyone could understand:

Stop borrowing.

Repay the present debt.

Reduce the cost of government.

In 1801 the national debt was about eighty million dollars. The government's annual income was over ten million dollars. The new plan set aside money for interest and for some payments on the debt; it stopped excise taxes (a tax that Americans had to pay on some of their own products); and it proposed to spend less on the army and the navy.

Most citizens thought that the new plan was good, and all citizens were pleased about lower taxes. The United States prospered. At the end of a year the debt was less. It seemed likely that in a few years it would be paid; then the government could use tax money for roads, bridges, and canals that would help everyone. Government finances were going well.

But trouble developed in Jefferson's own party. When John Adams had appointed judges and other federal officers from his party, Republicans were annoyed, but not deeply concerned. They thought that as soon as Jefferson's administration was under way, he would put the Federalists out. Months passed, and the President had done no such thing. Republicans came to the White House to protest.

"Republicans won the election," they said. "Republicans should have the jobs."

"I cannot discharge a man for his political beliefs," the President answered. "Show me where a man fails in his duty, and I shall see that such a one goes."

"Oh, some are good, some bad. But they are Federalists."

"I feel for you," Jefferson admitted. "I believe that government jobs should be divided between parties in the same proportion that voters were divided in the last election. As fast as men resign, or die, or prove unfit I shall work toward that ratio." Visitors hardly bothered to hide their anger. They knew that such natural changes would come slowly. Actually, at the end of Jefferson's first term half the appointive jobs were still held by Federalists.

Perhaps the President suffered most, in those Adams appointments, from the serious friction between himself and Chief Justice Marshall. Jefferson wished to keep a perfect balance of power among the three parts of government—legislative, executive, and judicial. Marshall, as Chief Justice, took for the court the final decision over legislative and executive acts.

Jefferson had three reasons for fearing this power of the court; judges were appointed, not elected by the people; they held office for life; and impeachment was difficult.

But Marshall was there. The President could only do his best with the problem Adams had created for him.

The President enjoyed a happy summer visit at Monticello, and in the late fall Martha and her children came for a visit in the White House. She was a skillful hostess and very popular. Later, Maria and her little son Francis visited him, too. Maria was beautiful, and Washingtonians loved her.

"I cannot stay long, Papa," she said affectionately. "You must come to Virginia." She was happiest at home.

Soon the wisdom of Jefferson's economy with the army and navy was severely tested by a foreign power.

Along the shores of the Mediterranean were several small nations hardly known to Americans—Algiers, Tunis, Tripoli, Morocco. These had laid tribute, pirate fashion, on shipping. European powers had paid rather than fight; American ships did the same. But the more they paid, the more was demanded. In 1801 the Pasha of Tripoli decided he was not getting enough.

"The tribute paid to me from that last American ship is worth less than the present they gave to the Bey of Tunis!" he cried furiously. "We'll show those Americans!" He had the American flagpole at the consulate hacked down as a declaration of war.

Rulers of the other small countries watched to see what America would do.

Jefferson sent four ships to teach Tripoli to respect the United States. Orders said, "You are not to land and make war. You are to patrol the coast." When a pirate's ship crossed their course, Americans boarded and dismantled her without a shot. Then they set her free to get home as best she could.

For months after that, boys in the United States thrilled over the tales of American heroes, as Preble, Eaton, and the brave men with them taught respect for America. Finally, in 1805, Tripoli made a treaty that had a wholesome effect on the other countries.

All this time, Jefferson thought often about the West, especially that vast part called Louisiana. Most Americans were busy earning a living and had little interest in that part of the country—except perhaps in the Mississippi River. That was the highway to market for hundreds of enterprising settlers. Even they felt little concern about the government of Louisiana. Spain owned it, and she was too weak to make trouble.

During his first year in the White House, Jefferson heard that Spain had secretly given Louisiana to Napoleon. That changed the situation. Jefferson called Madison into conference at once.

"We have not enough ships or troops to fight," Jefferson said thoughtfully. "We might ally ourselves with England— but you know, Jemmy, we don't want that."

"An alliance against France, no," Madison agreed. "But the owner of New Orleans is a potential enemy."

Jefferson took a knife from his pocket and began to sharpen

a quill pen. "The day Napoleon's troops land in New Orleans, that very day we marry the English fleet. We might write to Robert." Robert Livingston was the American minister to France. "I can tell him that the French possession of New Orleans will force us to get a navy and forge the first cannon to fire against Europe." Both men sat silent.

"We do not want this," Jefferson went on. "I shall make that plain. But France may force us to action."

The letter was written—an amazing document in which Jefferson daringly threatened the great Napoleon. He also asked for the purchase price of New Orleans.

Some time later, news that France owned New Orleans burst upon Americans. Letters poured onto Jefferson's desk.

"Are American crops to float into the arms of France?"

"What shall we do with our harvests? We can't lug them across the Alleghenies, can we?"

"Settlers won't go west now—that's sure!"

Boatmen on the Ohio were stopped for news.

"What's President Jefferson doing about this?"

"Nothing, I reckon," boatmen shouted back.

But the President was acting boldly, though quietly. He asked Congress to appropriate two million dollars for international use. Then he sent James Monroe to France to help Livingston buy New Orleans. These were daring and unprecedented actions.

While Monroe was still on the ocean, Napoleon was taking stock of his military equipment; he needed more, but lacked cash. He sent his minister of foreign affairs to talk with Livingston.

"How much will you pay for Louisiana?" the minister asked.

"We had not considered that!" Livingston was dismayed.

"You'd better buy while you can. How much will you pay?"

Livingston had no orders, but he named a figure.

"Too low. Think it over and bid again!" the minister said.

Monroe arrived the next morning; and after a conference, the two Americans called at the French foreign office. Soon arrangements were settled for the United States to buy Louisiana from France. The cost was about fifteen million dollars.

In due time, Congress approved the treaty of sale.

France made a colorful ceremony of the actual transfer at New Orleans on December 20th, 1803. There, for the first time, the Stars and Stripes waved over the new territory, which was twice the size of the original thirteen states.

This region was now open to settlers, and by terms of the treaty, the inhabitants were to be American citizens "as soon as possible." Many thought Jefferson would set up the American form of government at once.

But Jefferson believed that people must earn a free government; changing a name was not enough. American citizens needed to feel acquainted with their new possession, too. He sent Lewis and Clark up the Missouri, into the Northwest. The aim was to find a route to the Pacific Ocean. On the journey they were guided by the Indian "Bird Woman," and with her help succeeded in their mission.

About the same time Zebulon Pike explored the Mississippi and then went on west to the Rockies. Americans, and especially their President, eagerly awaited reports from these explorers.

Jefferson was praised for the quick decisions that resulted in getting this new territory for his country. Admirers wrote

asking for the date of his birth that it might be made a national holiday. To this he replied:

> "I have always declined letting my birthday be known. If you wish a celebration, choose the date of your country's birth, July 4, 1776."

During that winter, praise for Jefferson and his party was so general that Federalists were startled. New Englanders, in particular, began to fear that their businesses were threatened by the growth of the West. There was even talk of New England seceding from the Union.

"We've had enough of rule by Virginians!" some said.

About this time, the country was threatened in another way. Vice-President Aaron Burr had long been disgruntled. Now he made a plan to gain power for himself. He would organize the Southwest into a confederacy with himself as governor. The name was a blind; he expected to be a king.

Jefferson kept silent, though he knew about this. The relationship with his Vice-President was certainly awkward; he thought it best to bide his time.

Other anxieties plagued him that winter, and Maria was ill. In February her daughter was born, but Maria's health was no better. Letters from Virginia kept the President uneasy.

Spring was blossoming over the hills of Virginia when a rider pulled up at the White House steps.

"You are to come, sir! Miss Maria is very ill!" he said.

Jefferson went to Monticello by the fastest relay of horses. He was in time to see that everything possible was done for beautiful Maria—and that it was all in vain. She died in April, the season she loved best.

When the President's sorrow became known, hundreds of letters came to him. One, in particular, brought him comfort: Mrs. John Adams had learned to love little Polly during her short stay in London, years before, and now mourned her early death. Her letter led to a reconciliation between Adams and Jefferson, two great Americans who had once been good friends. This time, their friendship endured.

That same spring, Burr, still Vice-President, decided to run for the office of governor of New York. He counted on Federalists and dissatisfied Republicans to support him. But Hamilton still distrusted Burr; he worked successfully to defeat him.

Burr was furious! He challenged Hamilton to a duel and ruthlessly shot him. Americans were revolted by this wanton act. Burr's political influence was ended for a time.

In the autumn of 1804, the country was prosperous and President Jefferson seemed popular with the whole nation. Taxes had been lowered, and the debt was being paid. Louisiana had been acquired without war. Jefferson was easily elected on this record, with George Clinton of New York as Vice-President; his party won fifteen out of the seventeen states.

Jefferson's decisive victories in two elections were accomplished without speeches or campaign promises. He won because his quiet work, by letters and articles, had convinced the majority of the people that he had faith in them, that he was interested in their welfare. They answered by giving him the highest office in the land.

The growing Federal City looked a little better for that second inauguration, though it was still a morass of mud. Jefferson took the oath of office March 4, 1805, and made a short address, accounting for his stewardship. He pointed out that the country seemed united and that it was his hope that the public servants would "secure for you the peace, friendship, and approbation of all nations."

Unfortunately this fine political weather did not last. Burr seemed determined to wreck the United States. The President at first tried to ignore his reported plans. It seemed incredible that Burr should succeed in building a great western empire. But soon the man's treason went so far that Jefferson ordered his arrest.

The prisoner was brought to Richmond for trial and there, amazingly, society made a hero of him. Judge Marshall was a guest at a dinner for Burr the evening before he was to preside at the trial.

This trial was more of a legal battle between political enemies than an effort to bring a traitor to justice. Burr was freed. But outraged public opinion forced him to leave his country.

Foreign affairs were troubling the President, too. In their own quarrels, England and France each tried to end American trade with the other. France stopped American ships in mid-ocean. England stopped and boarded American ships and dragged off sailors she claimed were deserters; they were given no chance to prove their American citizenship.

Caught between those two European powers, citizens of the United States angrily called for war.

Thomas Jefferson saw political affairs in human terms. Naturally Americans had their pride—but war brought grief and misery. If American ships would stay at home, he thought, perhaps need for war would pass. He proposed a bill called the Embargo Act, which ordered foreign trade stopped.

"He seems to be remembering the 'Non-Importation Act' of before the Revolutionary War," some remarked.

"Such an idea will never work, now," others said. "The country is very different today from what it was in 1769."

The Act made trouble from the start. Factories closed. Shipbuilding stopped. Farm prices dropped. Business restrictions destroyed many liberties people had enjoyed.

But Jefferson noticed that speech was still quite free. He got hundreds of letters blaming him for the nation's troubles.

One morning a friend chanced to see a letter on the President's desk. He flushed angrily at the words he read.

"This shouldn't be allowed!" he cried hotly.

"That letter comforts me," Jefferson said quietly. "I wish the writer did not hate me. But I rejoice that he can express himself without fear. As long as a citizen has the right to speak his mind, our essential freedoms are safe."

Soon Jefferson came to see that for two reasons the Embargo Act was not succeeding. First, the United States had become dependent upon foreign trade; when it stopped, her own people suffered as much as the enemy. Second, this personal hardship prevented united support of the Act—and without the support of all, it must fail.

Jefferson talked with leaders about what to do. To Meriwether Lewis he wrote: "If our foreign affairs do not clear up, war may be better than the embargo." His opinion seemed to be changing; to another friend he wrote: "I think one war is enough for a lifetime. Still, if it becomes necessary, we must meet it like men."

As the time for the election of 1808 drew near, Federalists campaigned against the embargo. Republicans pointed out that even if war came, the embargo had given the nation time to prepare. They begged Jefferson to accept the nomination for President.

"No! Eight years is enough for one man—perhaps too much!" He was very firm. "I shall not run again."

So it was James Madison and George Clinton who were elected that November. Republicans had a comfortable margin of votes in spite of the embargo disputes.

One of Jefferson's last official duties was to abolish that Act. He was glad that it had been tried; men should always try to settle differences without war. Someday, he confidently believed, a way would be found for men to live together without bloodshed.

chapter seventeen

Thomas Jefferson Returns Home

WASHINGTON, THE CAPITAL CITY of the United States, had improved in the eight years since Thomas Jefferson was first inaugurated. Some streets had been cleared of stumps; but the March mud was still deep. Houses had been built, and some progress made on the Capitol.

When Jefferson and Madison met there on March 4, 1809, the incoming President glanced at his friend, puzzled.

"You appear gay as a schoolboy," he said, a bit testily.

"To me, this seems a very solemn occasion."

"For you, maybe it is," Jefferson agreed, and his eyes gleamed happily. "But for me, the boy is getting out of school. Naturally he is lighthearted."

"I feel aged," Madison sighed. "A hundred maybe."

"But you are only fifty-eight," Jefferson reminded him, amused. "You are just the age I was eight years ago when I walked from Conrad's boardinghouse to take the oath. We had solemn problems then, Jemmy," he added.

"I know," Madison agreed, more cheerfully. "And you met them ably. With your help, I shall try not to fail my country. But today I ask myself, 'Why did they choose me?'"

"Because you are an honest man, a loyal patriot, and devoted to the republican form of government—reasons enough for election. And now, here we are."

Before and after the ceremony of inauguration, the two men were acclaimed by the crowds. Madison had been elected by a comfortable margin in spite of the Embargo Act. Its repeal was sure to satisfy most voters.

At the Inaugural Ball that evening, guests noticed that Jefferson was witty, even gay. Many a beauty eyed him regretfully. Few had guessed this rarely-seen side of his complex personality.

Martha Jefferson Randolph had come to Washington to help her father pack. She found it a big task. Jefferson's secretary had been working for days, separating personal from government correspondence. Now White House aides carried armfuls of papers to the room where Martha was packing.

"Papa!" she called as Jefferson passed the door. "Is all this to go? The coach cannot possibly carry so much!"

"Um-m-m," Jefferson entered and looked at the piles. "I have written and received so many letters!" He wandered around, looking at the papers and sizing up the empty chests assembled.

"These do not need to go by coach," he decided. "I can ship them to Richmond and from there by barge to Shadwell. Yes, I need all this at Monticello. As I have time I shall sort and index it. These papers will make a good record of our times. But you must not tire yourself, my dear. I shall send a man to help you."

Now and then, as Martha continued packing, she paused to notice some of his treasures. The little testament from which her father had read to them evenings stirred her memory.

"I remember when Father was working on this, early in his Presidency," she said to the aide who had come to help. "He clipped verses that told the story of Jesus and pasted them in narrative sequence. He said that some day he meant to study that story in various languages. He believed the words of Jesus, 'Love the Lord thy God and thy neighbor as thyself,' were the sum of all religion." Tenderly she packed the little book in her own bag.

Another heap of papers seemed to have Indian words.

"These must be the Indian vocabularies Father told me to watch for," she said. "For years, oh, perhaps from his youth, my father has collected Indian words as other men collect dollars. I heard him say, once, that if he could get together two hundred and fifty words, naming common things, in each of many dialects, he might discover a common origin."

The aide looked at the papers with alert interest.

"I have heard," he said, "that your father was trying to prove that the Indian languages came from Russia—"

"You have been misinformed," Martha interrupted. "Father never tries to *prove* anything. He is open-minded when he investigates. He gets facts; then he studies to see what the facts reveal." She looked at the chests carefully. "This is a stout box—the Indian papers will be safe in it."

She packed letters connected with her father's work as president of the American Philosophical Society and reports from Meriwether Lewis, along with seeds, leaves, bits of rocks, and soil from the West. At home these would go in the case with similar trophies Jefferson had brought from Europe.

Finally all was done. Martha drove home in a coach. Jefferson stayed for a few last duties, saw his boxes on the ship, and then mounted his horse and departed. A violent snowstorm made it a hard journey; he was more than ever glad when at last he rounded the mountain and saw his beautiful home.

He had declined the celebration his neighbors wished to give on his return, but as soon as his writing desk was unpacked he wrote them a note of appreciation of their friendship.

One sad loss marked the move from Washington to Monticello. In due time the boxes packed in the White House reached Monticello, and the overseer checked them in.

"Twenty-nine, safe and in good condition," he reported.

"I thought there were thirty," Martha Randolph said, her forehead puckered with concern. "Every one is valuable; do count again." The count, twenty-nine, was confirmed. So Jefferson was called to see what was missing.

"That heaviest box," he found. "The one with my Indian vocabulary studies. Send back at once and trace the whole way."

Trusted servants went by canoe down the Rivanna, down the James. Above Richmond they noticed trampled grass and bits of paper on the bank. They landed—and found the chest, empty. After some detective work they got this story.

New wharfhands had moved the boxes from the ship to the river barge at Richmond.

"Who-all these belong to?" one asked.

"Some rich man, going to the mountains."

"This box must be full of gold; it's heavy enough," another said, and his eyes glistened greedily.

Up the river, out of sight, they turned ashore, opened that box—and found it full of papers. Their greed thwarted, they angrily tore the sheets and tossed them to the winds. The Monticello men gathered up a few, rainsoaked and muddy.

"Can you set down what you remember, Papa?" Martha's voice was tender as she saw his disappointment.

"Remembered words might not be accurate, Daughter. I guess that project was never to be."

Later, a language scholar heard of those papers and asked the privilege of studying them. Jefferson sent the muddied sheets but they were of little use. His long study was lost.

As spring came on, Jefferson settled into a daily routine of living. Before breakfast he read and wrote letters. During the morning he inspected his shops and fields and the changes he was constantly making on the house.

In the afternoon he gave himself to the children. All the remaining years of his life there were children at Monticello. Martha's family of eleven boys and girls grew up there. The younger ones were still romping about when the older Randolphs brought great-grandchildren to visit. The Carrs brought grandnieces and grandnephews; Francis Eppes, Maria's son, was often there.

Thomas Jefferson enjoyed directing their education; he suggested books to read, listened to their talk, answered their questions, and allowed them to watch as he installed various interesting and useful gadgets.

After the three o'clock dinner the children had their play hour when Thomas Jefferson belonged to them alone. If the weather was good, they had walks or games on the lawn.

"Grandpa!" James or Benjamin or Francis might call. "Come be umpire. We want to race." Jefferson hurried down the steps, bushy gray hair fluttering, his brown coat and green stockings blending into the landscape as children of assorted ages lined up on the west lawn awaiting his signal.

"Ready?" he called to them.

"All set!" the boys would answer, as girls gathered up long skirts and took deep breaths.

"Go!" he called, as the white handkerchief fluttered from his hand and touched the grass.

On rainy days they played indoor games, the children taking turns in choosing their favorites.

"It's my turn today, Grandpa," Ellen announced. "I choose 'I love my love with an A' because I have a new word."

"Then you will read, Grandpa?" Francis begged, and Jefferson nodded his promise.

When their grandfather's voice grew weary, or when candles were lighted, the children slipped away. Then Jefferson opened his own book.

He had time for adults, too. In summer the Monticello

coach fetched sister Anna for an annual visit on the mountain, a rest and a treat for her. Thomas Jefferson continued his watchful care over her twin brother, too. Their guardian had died when Randolph was twelve and Thomas, twenty-four. The young lad was sent to college; and he studied music. Later he served in the Revolution.

Randolph had none of the keen mental drive of his famous brother, but he had stalwart sons who carried on the Jefferson name. Thomas and Randolph corresponded about horses and dogs, tools and seed, fishing and harness. They lived only twenty miles apart, but the journey was a difficult one, seldom undertaken. The letters were a help to Randolph in his farming and other labors.

One summer Thomas had a spare spinning jenny for a time, and he wrote to Randolph about it:

> " . . . while it is here it offers good opportunity for your spinner to learn upon it. After it is gone there will be no idle machine for a learner to practice on. She had better come immediately."

Randolph sent the girl, and after seeing her started at the spinning jenny, Thomas wrote about her progress:

> "It will take her some days according to her aptness . . . she must continue to spin, here, that she may be more perfect. With affectionate salutations
>
> Th. Jefferson"

Other kinsfolk and friends came to visit, too, and were taken into the family circle. President Madison visited when he was in Virginia; James Monroe rode over from Ashlawn, three miles away, and lingered for a day or two of talk.

Alas! There were still other visitors. Far too many. No one, Jefferson least of all, had anticipated one result of his public service that deeply affected his life after retirement. Thomas Jefferson was a famous man now, and scores, hundreds, thousands of people came to see him.

George Washington had been plagued with visitors at Mount Vernon. Now hordes climbed the mountain uninvited to see the writer of the Declaration of Independence. There was no inn nearby; so, arrived there, they stayed. Many were devoted to the ideals he believed in; many were merely curious. How was a Virginia gentleman to turn them away? He felt he must receive them. Often the house was overrun.

One day Jefferson chanced to go into his dining room, and there he found a group of strangers. One man was fumbling along the paneling.

"I heard you had a contrivance in the wall," he said, with no apology for having walked into the house.

Graciously Jefferson opened a panel, pulled a rope, and drew up a set of shelves. The visitors stared in delight.

"It brings things from the basement—is that right?" one asked. "What do you call it?"

"Well, at first it had no name," Jefferson replied politely. "But as long as we have had the thing, it has never talked back. So I call it a 'dumb waiter.'"

Visitors wandered into his bedroom and admired his

chaise longue, a novelty then. They saw his bed that pulled up out of the way in the daytime. They looked at his letter press, his polygraph and drawing table, the folding ladder, and the great clock over the front door, all designed by Jefferson.

Visitors were greeted with politeness—but they became a burden. Martha stayed at Monticello most summers to be hostess for her father. One day he drew her aside and whispered anxiously, "How many are there this evening, Daughter?"

"Fifty. I have just counted them. Don't ask me where I shall sleep them all—I don't know yet. But don't you worry, Papa. I shall manage." Somehow she always did.

As years went by, the visitors continued; they became a heavy drain upon Monticello. They ate food that should have gone to market; wore out chairs and sheets. And Thomas Jefferson was not the rich planter they considered him. He was struggling to pay debts incurred during the war and in long years of serving his country.

Though he lived on a distant mountain, letters received kept Jefferson in close touch with national and world events. He was deeply disturbed when war came in 1812. And later when the British invaded and burned Washington, he took action.

"The Congressional Library is burned!" he exclaimed to his daughter. "Our congressmen need books. I shall write at once offering my own library to them."

"Can you spare it, Papa?"

"They need it," was his only reply. He wrote that letter

at once, in September of 1814, explaining that he had between nine and ten thousand volumes, all well bound; that the sections on parliamentary law and diplomacy were very good.

> "I enclose a catalogue," he wrote. "They may be valued by persons named by themselves [Congress] and payment made convenient. They may enter into immediate use of it as eighteen or twenty wagons would place it in Washington in a fortnight."

Congress haggled shamefully; the offer was not accepted for several months. And then they paid $23,950—less than half the cost. These books became the foundation of the Library of Congress. As for Jefferson, he began at once building a new library. He could not live without books.

So, with events both happy and troublesome, life at Monticello went on. In spite of rainy seasons and visitors, some old debts were paid. The children were growing and learning to enjoy reading. Life was good. In a letter to John Adams, Jefferson wrote, "I steer my bark with Hope in the head, leaving Fear a-stern. I am happy in what is around me."

chapter eighteen

Wise Man of the Mountain

ALL HIS LIFE, Thomas Jefferson was interested in education.
He directed the studies of many young people in his family and
among his friends. He planned schools for all children, because
he believed that a free government was secure only when its
citizens were educated.

A few days after he became governor of Virginia, Jefferson's
bill for education had been presented to the assembly. For
fifteen years it was debated—but it was not passed. Undaunted,

he never lost interest or faith that someday all boys and girls would be able to get as much education as each wanted or could use.

He longed for common schools in every county, for good secondary schools for those who wished for more education. And to top the program, he hoped for a fine state university. His opportunity to attain this last came unexpectedly.

On a spring day in 1814, he rode into Charlottesville on an errand. As he passed Stone Tavern, he saw five friends talking together by the hitchrack, and he waved to them.

"Stop with us awhile, Mr. Jefferson," one of the men called. "Perhaps you can advise us." Jefferson dismounted, hitched Eagle, his favorite horse, and joined them.

"We think of setting up a school," one told him. "We should like to have our boys educated near home."

"The population of Albemarle County has so increased," another added, "that we need an academy here."

Jefferson's eyes gleamed, but his manner was casual.

"Why plan merely an academy?" he asked. "Why not have a college? Call it Central College. Charlottesville is near the center of our beautiful state."

The men looked dazed; they had not dreamed so high. But as Jefferson put it to them, why not? Especially as he volunteered to work at raising the necessary money.

While raising funds, Jefferson again worked out a plan for education. He sent it to the chairman of the project, Peter Carr, the nephew Jefferson loved and whose own education he had directed years before. In this plan Jefferson spoke of his earlier hopes for public education and set down his ideas for higher training.

When the trustees of Central College were appointed, Thomas Jefferson was named their leader. The cornerstone of the first building in Charlottesville was laid in 1817. By this date, the state legislature had grown interested. Jefferson's dreams were still far ahead of all others. He was now planning for a University of Virginia.

In February of 1818, the assembly of Virginia authorized a state university and set a meeting for August at Rockfish Gap. The location of the university was to be selected then.

Jefferson knew that Staunton, Lexington, and Richmond would each want the university; so he arrived early—and ready.

"Jemmy, I thought you would come," he said, as ex-President Madison rode up.

"James, this is good of you to take the time," he remarked, as he greeted President Monroe at the low doorway.

A gathering of such distinction in this modest tavern was a rare sight. A President, two ex-Presidents, judges, legislators, and others sat side by side. Jefferson, tall, lean, and alert, was easily the leader to whom all turned.

Claims and invitations were read. Then Jefferson showed them a map of Virginia which he had cut from cardboard. On it, near the center, was Charlottesville, proof of its claims. The twenty-one men studied that map, and then sixteen voted for Charlottesville. Jefferson's map had won his point.

That meeting continued during four days. It was decided to call the institution the University of Virginia and to have all studies elective. Thomas Jefferson was made rector (the title meant chief director), and he was asked to work out details —designs for buildings, courses, faculty.

"Gentlemen, you have given me work very much to my liking," he told them, and his face glowed with pleasure. "I shall see that we progress as fast as possible. Already I have a plan in mind—buildings of warm brick trimmed with stone columns, built around three sides of an open square. I pledge you my word that it will be beautiful." Then the meeting adjourned.

Later, in his report to the legislature, Jefferson set down objectives that were timeless. In part he wrote that a university's purpose is

> to form statesmen, legislators, and judges on whom public prosperity and individual happiness are so much to depend
>
> to expound the principles of government
>
> to harmonize agriculture, manufacturers, and commerce
>
> to develop the reasoning faculties of our youth
>
> to enlighten them and administer to the health and comforts of human life

The charter was granted, and work began. Jefferson's days were now full of business. Nail and brick factories were set up; marble was ordered from Italy; ground was leveled; and with the help of Monticello men, Jefferson himself surveyed the ground and staked out the first building.

Jefferson still admired the art of Palladio, the architect whose drawings had inspired the designs of Monticello. But the university buildings were worked out in a style of his own, adapted to the new conditions and uses.

The work went in spurts; sometimes well, sometimes dragging for lack of funds. Then Jefferson had to go out and raise more money. Construction cost much more than was expected; and in the depression which followed the war, conditions were bad for raising money, especially in a farm state.

Jefferson's own affairs suffered in this depression. Fine crops were hard to sell at any price. There was no market for land. His finances never recovered from the difficulties of this long depression after the end of the War of 1812.

Through these busy years, Jefferson wrote more than usual. He was asked to set down the story of his own life and of the famous men he had known. He complied, for he saw that few were living then who could tell the true happenings of Revolutionary days and the early fight for freedom.

He even managed to finish that little Bible, as he had long planned. He pasted parallel columns of Jesus's story side by side on a page—Greek, Latin, English, and French. How different the words looked; yet the story was the same.

Fortunately, Jefferson had most of this work completed by 1822, for in that year he had a serious accident. He was going down the terrace steps at Monticello to mount Eagle when a support gave way and threw him. His left arm was broken and never again gave good service for writing. His right arm, broken years earlier, was stiff and painful; he had been using his left hand. After this accident, writing was never again the pleasure it had been.

But the building of the university went on. Burwell, the trusted successor to Jupiter, brought old Eagle around every morning and helped his master mount. Once ahorse, Jefferson set off by himself for Charlottesville. After dinner, he strolled on the terrace and kept an eye on the work through a telescope he had set up.

In the midst of all this interesting labor, an unexpected event gave Thomas Jefferson the greatest pleasure. Lafayette sailed across the sea to visit America. He landed in New York in August of 1824 and was greeted with an ovation.

To Jefferson's delight, Lafayette wrote that he was coming to visit at Monticello. A letter of greeting was sent off posthaste. Jefferson wrote another letter, too; this went to a friend in Congress. In it, Jefferson wrote that he believed Lafayette's visit would help foster a friendly feeling between the two republics, France and the United States. Then he added, "I hope we shall close it with something more solid for him than dinners and balls." Congress acted on this suggestion and voted Lafayette $200,000 and some land, "for his important services and expenditures during the American revolution."

The day came when autumn colors decked the trees of Monticello and martial music echoed on the mountains; Lafayette was nearing Monticello.

"I must go to meet him," Jefferson exclaimed.

"No, stay by the door; we have planned everything," friends said. So Jefferson waited.

The music grew louder—then softer. Weren't they coming to the east door? No. For now the music was from the west.

Jefferson hurried to the door that opened onto the wide lawn as the cavalcade rounded the corner of Honeymoon Cottage and the carriage with Lafayette came into view.

Lafayette saw his old friend hurrying down the steps. He halted the carriage, got out, and rushed across the lawn.

"Jefferson! *Mon ami!*" he cried.

"Lafayette!" The two embraced in the affectionate French fashion. Hats came off, and tears glistened in many an eye

at the moving scene. Then the music resumed, and the two men linked arms and strolled to the mansion.

Lafayette stayed for several days. Jefferson kept open house for the friends who came to see him, and there was an elegant banquet in the largest finished building on the university campus. It was one of the very happy weeks of Jefferson's long life.

A few months later, March 7, 1825, the University of Virginia was formally opened. Students and faculty were assembled; enough buildings were finished for immediate use, and the rest were nearing completion. This was another red-letter day for the happy founder.

Thomas Jefferson had enjoyed good health most of the eighty-three years of his life. But after he passed his April birthday in the year 1826, he knew that his work was nearly finished. His life ended on the day that he said was more important than his own birth date—July Fourth.

His country had grown and strengthened in the fifty years since he wrote the Declaration of Independence. Now he left it to posterity.

Few men have rivaled Thomas Jefferson's many skills. He was lawyer, architect, musician, botanist, farmer, philosopher, and politician—the greatest creative genius of his time. He designed a home, a capitol, a university; those, people could see. But his greatest work was as designer of a plan for a government of and by free men.

Time is needed for good building. When Dabney Carr and Tom Jefferson roamed the mountains, a vision of a house on a mountain formed in Tom's mind. Years passed before the first brick was set; through more years the house grew.

Even so it was with his larger work. While he was a lawyer and burgess, a vision of a free society began to form in Thomas Jefferson's mind. His Declaration of Independence was a blueprint of the kind of nation men might have—if they had the courage and the wisdom. It would need both.

In this document he wrote that all men are created equal —what did those words mean? He had only to think of his own family to see inequalities. Of the ten children of strong Peter and gentle Jane Jefferson, two died in infancy, Mary and Lucy were average, Elizabeth, simple-minded, Jane and Martha, intelligent, the twins hardly able to cope with living, and Thomas a genius. Certainly they were not "equal." Yet under a free government each could live and have an equal chance to make what each would of nature's gifts.

Thomas Jefferson saw, too, that freedom *from* something is not enough; freedom must be *for* something. War might free the colonies from England. But only when they learned to rule themselves would men be free for the kind of life they might create for all.

Jefferson realized that freedom is dangerous. In a free land a man may attain whatever height he can; but he is also free to fail. A government that protects a man from failure also, by exactly that much, restricts success. Jefferson's faith in people made him believe that men did not want coddling and protection. He offered freedom—not as a goal, but as a path to a better life.

Some of Jefferson's later writings show that he may have wondered how people in the years to come might remember him. After he died, his family found a paper on which Jefferson had written what he thought should be inscribed on the stone by his grave. It said:

HERE WAS BURIED

THOMAS JEFFERSON

AUTHOR OF THE DECLARATION OF AMERICAN INDEPENDENCE

OF THE STATUTE OF VIRGINIA FOR RELIGIOUS FREEDOM

& FATHER OF THE UNIVERSITY OF VIRGINIA.

In the years since that Fourth of July, 1826, people have come to think of him, too, as the champion of the common people. They see that though he was an idealist who lived upon a mountain, he understood men and dreamed of a government for men of all races, creeds, and economic levels, so designed that each should enjoy equality of opportunity—the one equality within the gift of government.

He left this dream to his countrymen. Only time can tell what use they will make of their noble heritage from Thomas Jefferson.